Film Noir: The Best Of The Classics

T.S.GARP

T.S.Garp

DEDICATION

The book is dedicated to all my friends in the entertainment industry. I was once part of the new generation of filmmakers and young screenwriters back in the 1990s during that great era of independent filmmakers that helped launched the careers of Quentin Tarantino and Robert Rodriguez. This book is dedicated to my old alumni of indie filmmakers, actors, and writers, a great group of guys and gals that love all types of film genre, and the craft of filmmaking.

Film Noir: The Best of The Classics

INTRODUCTION

This book came about during my study of film history and a film genre that has always fascinated me, film noir. There are so many depths to film noir and that it has the ability to crossover into almost any other genre or subject matter. For almost twenty years, beginning in 1941 with what is considered the very first film noir, *The Maltese Falcon*, classic film noir has had a strong presence and influence on mainstream cinema. The primary themes and character types, displayed in these moody, dark films, often reflect the social and psychological state of the general populace of the 1940s and 1950s. My research resulted in several essays on the subject and revealed some interesting historical facts, film production concepts, techniques, directors, cinematographers, writers, and the variety of actors that became famous in this explosive classic genre.

The basis of film noir stems from silent motion pictures and German Expressionism of the 1920s. A stylistic mixture of light and shadow, these black and white movies were visually stunning combined with brilliant writing from crime thriller novels boasting cynical detectives, femme fatales, and a slew of killers. There is a vast difference from watching a regular film versus a film noir, from the narrative, action, camerawork, editing, characters with ambiguous morals, hidden agendas, and skewed motivations, all walking a fine line between good and evil, in a world filled with snappy dialogue, eerie locations, murder, mysteries, and plot twists. What makes classic film noir so interesting is that it came from a bygone era that perfectly illustrates the best example of creativity with compelling storylines, layered motifs, and innovative filmmaking that has broken new ground in this particular movement in film history that is still influencing cinema even today.

T.S.Garp

CONTENTS

Dedication		3
Introduction		4
1	The Maltese Falcon	6
2	Cat People	13
3	Double Indemnity	22
4	Detour	27
5	The Big Sleep	32
6	Out of The Past	40
7	The Third Man	50
8	Gun Crazy	60
9	D.O.A.	69
10	In a Lonely Place	77
11	Kiss Me Deadly	85
12	The Big Heat	94
13	The Big Comb	105
14	Touch of Evil	114

1

THE MALTESE FALCON

A written narrative tells the backstory of the Knights Templars in 1539 had sent Charles V of Spain a Golden Falcon encrusted with rare jewels. But the Falcon was stolen by pirates and mysteriously vanished for 500 years. Enter today, the San Francisco detective agency of Spade and Archer are visited by a new client Miss Wonderly (Mary Astor). Sam Spade (Humphrey Bogart) meets the attractive Miss Wonderly first, she explains that she is searching for her missing sister who is with a dangerous man named Floyd Thursby. Miles Archer (Jerome Cowan) volunteers to follow Thursby that night and is murdered by an unseen assassin. Spade gets a call in the middle of the night informing him that his partner is dead. He arrives on the murder scene, police tell him Archer was shot once in the heart at close range. Spade's suspicions are peaked, tries to contact Miss Wonderly for answers, but she has checked out of her hotel, and vanished. He returns home and within minutes the local police show up, Detective Tom Polhaus (Ward Bond) and Lieutenant Dundy (Barton MacLane) are investigating the murder of Miles Archer. The Police reveal that Thursby, the man Archer was suppose to be trailing, was found dead, shot four times in the back. He maintains he has never seen Thursby before dead or alive, and offers a toast declaring "success to crime" ironically as he shares a drink with them.

The next morning Spade goes to his office where Archer's wife is waiting for him. Iva Archer (Gladys George) asked him straight-out did he kill her husband. He has been having an affair with Mrs. Archer, Spade is shocked by her question, and sends her away to meet later. His secretary Effie Prine (Lee Patrick) comes in and he gives her all the details like the widow thinks he murdered her husband and the cops think he killed Thursby. They are interrupted by a phone call from Miss Wonderly. She sends for Spade to her new location, without hesitation, he orders Effie to remove all traces of his partner's name and items from the office. Upon arriving at Miss Wonderly's place, Spade begins to question her, trying to get to the real truth. She confesses that she lied about her story, her name, and everything she told him before. Her real name is Brigid O'Shaughnessy, she begs for his help, fearful of the police finding her, but Spade isn't fooled by her "damsel in distress" routine. He sees right through her lies declaring, "now you are dangerous" and will continue working for her searching for clues for a higher fee.

Spade returns to his office and is visited by a short, impressively dressed man with the lingering scent of gardenias named Joel Cairo (Perter Lorre). He offers to hire Spade to locate a small black bird statue and is willing to pay him $5000 to get it. As Spade thinks it over, Mr. Cairo turns out to be a slippery fellow and pulls a gun on Spade, but the private eye is quicker, and disarmed him. When Cairo regains consciousness, they settle on a deal and Spade is paid $200 to retrieve the bird for Cairo's employer. Later he tells O'Shaughnessy about Cairo and another shady man following him. She is worried if she can trust him and Spade assures her with a kiss. They agree to meet Cairo at Spade's apartment and O'Shaughnessy informs them that she can get access to the bird in a few days. Spade pulls up a chair and watches them haggle over price when O'Shaughnessy reminds Cairo of something that happened in Instanbul, and this ignites an argument between them. Cairo is disarmed again by Spade as they hear a knock at the door. Spade goes out to greet them, but the continuing fight brings the police into his apartment. Quick thinking Spade, tells them it was a practical joke, no harm done, Cairo, and the police leave. O'Shaughnessy confesses all she knows about the Falcon.

The next morning at Cairo's hotel, Spade spots the guy that has been following him. Confronting him openly Spade learns his name is Wilmer Cook (Elisha Cook, Jr.) and is working for the Fat Man. He agrees to meet the Fat Man aka Kasper Gutman (Sydney Greenstreet), but Gutman reveals nothing to Spade. Undeterred, Spade informs the DA about what he knows, and they refuse to help. Later, Cook brings Spade back at Gutman's request to further discuss terms regarding the bird. Gutman explains the long history of the Maltese Falcon, a long lost treasure of a statue worth perhaps a up to $1,000,000, maybe more. They strike a deal if Spade can produce the bird, he says he can, but he is drugged, and awakens hours later. Spade is alone and after checking Gutman's room for clues he discovers a notice announcing the arrival of the ship La Paloma from Hong Kong. Spade rushes down there only to find the ship ablaze in flames.

Back at his office, he tells Effie what happened to him and suddenly a strange man staggered in holding a package, he collapses onto a couch, and dies. Spade checks him out, he is riddled with bullet holes, and discovers he is Captain Jacobi (Walter Huston) from the ship the La Paloma. The package contained the mysterious bird, O'shaughnessy calls, and Spade run over to her aid, bur first he stashes the Falcon at the bus depot for safe keeping. Spade is given a "bum steer" and can't locate O'Shaughnessy anywhere. Once inside Spade's place they are ambushed by Gutman, Cairo, and Cook. Gutman offers to pay Spade $10,000 to reveal the location of the Falcon. Spade agrees by counteroffering they need a "fall guy" to take the rap for the murders and nominates trigger-happy Cook. This idea infuriates Cook, but Spade and Cairo subdue him, knocking him unconscious.

They agree with Spade's plan and wait the long night until morning when he can retrieve the Falcon. Spade during this time demands to know the full truth and Gutman is happy to comply. Thursby and O'Shaughnessy had a close partnership and would not give up the bird easily, Cook killed Thursby and later O'Shaughnessy's other partner, Capain Jacobi. Gutman tells Spade

in secret to watchout for O'Shaughnessy for she is not to be trusted. By early morning Effie brings over the package, Spade places it on
his table, and like hungry animals Gutman, Cairo, and O'Shaughnessy rip it apart revealing the Maltese Falcon. Gutman scrapes on its surface and discover it is a fake. Totally devastated, they realize they were duped, Gutman takes back his money minus $1000 for Spade's fee. Cook vanished and Gutman and Cairo also depart. Spade notifies the police, tells them everything, and will wait for them to arrive at his place. He frantically interrogates O'Shaughnessy, demands the whole truth this time, she confesses that she did kill Archer, Spade is conflicted, but has no choice, he is going to turn her over to the police. Despite everything, the hard-boiled private eye has a code of ethics and sense of justice amidst murderers, liars, and betrayers.

The roots of how film noir came about on the screens of the cinema is as much a change in cinematic style as it is in a reflection of culture. The American public had been battered hard by the Great Depression of the 1930s and the Great Plain States had to endure tremendous hardships during the "Dust Bowl" period of severe drought. This era was also filled with notorious gangsters, crime, and corruption that was prominent on the public's mind. By the 1940s America was on the verge of war and anxieties were high. As Foster Hirsch observed in his book *The Dark Side of the Screen: Film Noir*, "in a number of ways, noir offers a symbolic social and psychological profile of the era" (Hirsch 19). The increasing outbreak of organized crime and pulp fiction in the 1920s and 1930s sowed the seeds for the film noir's inspiration. According to Foster Hirsch, "hard-boiled school of crime writing which flourished in the pages of pulp magazines in the twenties and thirties had a great impact on the noir tone" (Hirsch 24).

The dark allure of film noir is an artistic style all its own and a radical departure from conventional filmmaking. In their book *A Companion to Film Noir* authors Andre Spicer and Helen Hanson state that, "deep shadows, clutching hands, exploding revolvers, sadistic villains and heroines torment with deeply rooted diseases of the mind" (Spicer, Hanson 8). Known as the very first film noir, *The Maltese Falcon*, showcases all the primary elements that make up the genre such as the three main character types composing of the wry private eye, femme fatale, and memorable violent criminals.

Dashiell Hammett, author of *The Maltese Falcon*, had worked for the Pinkerton Detective Agency, which gave him ample experience and insight into some unsavory characters. Hammett was breaking new ground with his short stories and novels about cynical detectives. His influence greatly affected the genre to a whole new level, as noted by Hirsch, "Hammett chafed at the supposed limits of crime fiction, and he introduced motifs not previously associated with the genre. The feeling that something new and interesting is happening in Hammett's work is deepened in his novels, *Red Harvest, The Maltese Falcon, The Dain Curse,* and *The Glass Key*" (Hirsch 31). Hammett is known as a master of the mystery novel and highly acknowledged by other writers as an important influence on the hard-boiled detective genre.

Making his directorial debut, John Huston, a veteran screenwriter is set to direct *The Maltese Falcon* based on a novel by Dashiell Hammett, and Huston would write the screenplay himself. What makes *The Maltese Falcon* so important and memorizing are the collaboration between Huston and Humphrey Bogart. This one of a kind film would make both their careers in Hollywood and give new life to filmmaking that broke the mundane standard approach to this type of storyline, as noted by Spicer and Hanson, "classic film noir represents an attempt to break with those formulaic practices as Borde and Chaumenton and other French cineastes pointed out so early on" (Spicer, Hanson 18).

Together Huston and cinematographer Author Edeson, an expert in visionary conception, robust camera angles, and low key lighting set the overall moodiness for the film as observed by Hirsch, "the quiet chiaroscuro and occasional oblique angles of *The Maltese Falcon*" (Hirsch, 11). Even though Edeson had to work under the strict confines of the studio's "Hays Codes" of the 1930s, these constraints were enforced for nearly 40 years, had little influence on future film noir productions that would push the boundaries of the code. Huston's *The Maltese Falcon* was the third version of the film based on Hammett's book, Huston's style makes his version outstanding compared to the previous films, and Hirsch agrees, "directed by John Huston in a sedate manner, with only occasional low angles and theatrical lighting to call attention to the oddness of the characters" (Hirsch, 11.) Huston intuitively captured the essence of the times and subtle sinisterness of the players involved.

The femme fatale is Brigid O'Shaughnessy alias Ruth Wonderly, a sly manipulator and a pathological liar. A key characteristic trait of women in film noir, as explained by Hirsch, "as malevolent temptresses, their confined almost entirely to a sexual realm, their strength achieved only at the expense of men" (Hirsch 20). The main character in *The Maltese Falcon* is wisecracking protagonist, private eye Sam Spade, who is just doing his job, asserts Hirsch he is, "Hollywood's first hard-boiled hero, a brooding, tight-lipped loner who keeps his feelings to himself" (Hirsch 26). The film is laden with shady characters motivated by greed and violence. The incredibly obese antiquities/fortune hunter Kasper Gutman and his two gun-touting associates Joel Cairo and Wilmer Cook are all obsessed with obtaining the Falcon and immense wealth.

Amidst all the deception, greed, and violence, according to Hirsch, "Spade's speech to Brigid at the end is equally trenchant in its revelation of character. Spade tells Brigid that he has been wise to her from the beginning" (Hirsch 31). Despite the alluring temptation of wealth, Brigid's attractiveness, and his own contemptuous flaws, Spade manage to demonstrate his ability to walk a tight robe between crime and ethics. His true moral convictions are revealed at the end and steadfastly resolved by way of giving Brigid O'Shaughnessy a memorable speech about loyalty and partnership. Spade gives her a lesson in the hard-boiled code of honor and that despite his apparent love for her; she must pay the consequences for the murder of his partner Miles Archer.

Watching *The Maltese Falcon* you get a sense that you just stepped into a world full of dark shadows, violence, and shady characters involved in tale made up of plot twist, betrayal, and murder. No one is really, truly innocent as expressed by their dialog, dark humor, and utter cruelty to each other. And yet the portrayal of themes and human drama is expertly displayed by good actors with a good story and guided by a good director. The film holds up even today and is relevant to the era in which it was made and demonstrating that timeless tragic theme known as obsession. If anything, the moral message for audiences to take from *The Maltese Falcon* would be obsessions can lead you astray down a dark path into a world of blind veracity, where right and wrong are blurred, where no one is who they seem to be, and where one's desire is so fixated that nothing matters anymore, not even murder. The anti-hero Sam Spade in this masterpiece of filmmaking becomes the persona of all others in the film noir genre to come, where tough talking gumshoes follow a loyal code of loose ethics, and the women are fatal.

2

CAT PEOPLE

What makes *Cat People* terrifying is not so much of what you see, but rather what you don't see. The real terror comes from the shadows, sounds, and ancient lore. Despite the film's extremely low-budget, it still manages to effectively create a frightening and eerie atmosphere, and like most film noirs, is able to use everyday settings and turn them into places of mystery, fear, and death. At its core *Cat People* is a more a psychological horror film that plays on fears and superstition. The opening text that starts the film reminds us that evil is only sleeping and waiting to be set free to cause havoc. The passage reads, "Even as fog continues to lie in the valleys, so does ancient sin cling to the low places, the depressions in the world consciousness."

A beautiful and mysterious young woman named Irena Dubrovna (Simone Simon), in a New York City zoo catches the wondering eyes of admirer Oliver Reed (Kent Smith), an American marine engineer. He introduces himself as she sketches the likeness of the panther in the cage next to them (only her dawning has the panther impaled by a huge sword), they strike up a friendly conversation, Oliver instantly falls in love with her, learns she was born in Serbia, living New York as a fashion artist, and single. Irena is a solitary woman, having no friends, no visitors, and often sits alone, listening to the sounds of the nearby zoo in the darkness of her spacious apartment as comforting that would otherwise frighten most people. She even expresses feeling different from regular people and normally keeps to herself. Nevertheless, Oliver is intrigued by her innocent charm and mystery.

Irena warns him about an ancient and evil curse that befell her village hundreds of years ago, but nonetheless, has made her a victim of her Serbian heritage. Gradually, both Oliver and Irena's attractions for each other grows, and they quickly marry despite her misgivings, but the marriage begins to suffer immediately as Irena is opposed to consummating the marriage, no sex or affection is allowed. She informs her perplexed husband the reason is the curse, for it is mostly triggered by strong emotions like being aroused, and transforming her into a panther that would kill anyone nearby.

At first, Olivier is patient with Irena's emotional problem about showing too much affection, he buys a kitten to cheer her up, but the little creature is completely terrified of her, so he returns it back to the pet shop. He gives her a little bird instead to keep and this seems to work as the bird is in a cage, safe from Irena. But one day, Irena put her hand into the cage to play with the bird, and the bird instantly dies of fright, as if it knows all too well that Irena is something more than human, that she is a deadly beast composed of evil.

Oliver explains to her not to believe in such tales of witchcraft and black magic that seems to be haunting her. Thinking that it's all in her head, he sends her to see Dr. Louis Judd (Tom Conway), a roguish psychiatrist who is also attracted to Irena. The psychiatrist does seem to help Irena with her phobia at first, but her unhappy husband is already drifting into the arms of a coworker, Alice Moore (Jane Randolph), a friend who secretly loves him, whom he relates to as being a bit more "normal" type of woman than his untouchable new wife. Irena becomes consumed with jealousy over Alice, as her husband is spending more time with her, which is morally unethical for the husband to do rather than work out the problem with his wife. Irena's hopes for a good life are shattered, she feels she is losing Oliver to another woman as time goes on, and as her anger grows, Irena starts to succumb to the very fear she has been afraid with all her life.

Irena follows Alice late one night as Alice makes her way home, and as the rage fills Irena, the ancient curse takes over, and metamorphoses Irena into a deadly panther. Alice is sure she heard someone walking behind her in the spooky underpass and dim sidewalk, but she can see no one, and yet she can hear a faint sound of a growl getting nearer. The arriving city bus that picks up Alice saves her life and she departs swiftly. Later, on another night, Irena visits the health spa where Alice is swimming alone, and in cat form tries to terrorize her. As the lights mysteriously shut off, its all about the fear of the unknown, Alice can only hear the sound of a big cat stalking her on the deck, petrified, Alice screams for her life, and as help arrives, Irena quickly turns back on the lights.

The husband now seeks divorce, he has chosen Alice to be with, totally devastated, Irena reluctantly agrees. In a private meeting with Dr. Louis Judd, Oliver and Alice decide what to do about Irena. Oliver decides not to annul the marriage, but rather commit Irena for psychiatric care. Irena fails later to show up at another meeting to fully commit her to a hospital. Instead, when Oliver and Alice visit their office late the same night, Irena seeks to destroy them both in the darkness, only the sign of the Holy Cross (formed by Oliver grabbing a large drafting T-square) stops her from attacking them.

Irena meets with Dr. Louis Judd, who confesses his attraction to her, and gives her a fatal kiss on the lips. Afterwards, within seconds Irena transforms into a deadly panther, and attacks Dr. Louis Judd. The good doctor is always prepared; however, he quickly pulls out his hidden thin sword from his walking stick, and lashes out at the panther in defense. The vicious attack leaves the doctor dead on the floor. Oliver and Alice retrace Irena's steps, assuming she might be heading for the zoo. They arrive at the zoo in a haze of fog, find Irena dead on the ground near an open panther cage, she has been impaled by Dr. Louis Judd's sword. They both realize in that moment that the "cat people curse" is a real phenomenon and has claimed yet another victim, Irena.

Cat People is one of the first Hollywood films of the horror genre to play on the audience's fears rather than using gore or monsters. This horror-film noir perfectly illustrates that every culture firmly believes in the supernatural at one level or another, through our religion and customs, be it the Christian faith or belief in demons or monster of ancient lore, and the haunting aspects of "unnatural wickedness" which are firmly imbedded into our consciousness (much like Irena's), evoking fear of the unknown and sinful acts that are not tolerated. Indeed, in the film, Irena's plight is her insurmountable fear of her own heritage haunting her, getting married and having sex could spell disaster, as mentioned by writer John Grant in his book *A Comprehensive Encyclopedia of Film Noir: The Essential Reference Guide*, "she comes from a lineage of "cat people" - like werewolves, but shape shifting into cats rather than wolves - and fears that arousal might transform her in into a vicious panther" (Grant 111).

The excellent look, mood, and compelling story of the film are due in fact by three very creative people: Jacques Tourneur, Val Lewton, and Nicholas Musuraca. Beginning with the director of *Cat People* (1942) is Jacques Tourneur (1904 – 1977), an acclaimed French director of many classic film noir and low-budget horror films like *I Walked with a Zombie* (1943), *Out of the Past* (1947), *Berlin Express* (1948), and *Curse of the Demon* aka *Night of the Demon* (1957). Tourneur was born in France and came to America at a very young age, by adulthood; he entered the entertainment business of Hollywood, working first in silent pictures, and in the 1930s, started directing for major studios like MGM, Columbia, and RKO. His film career spans over 30 years long, *War-Gods of the Deep* (1964) a science fiction tale was his last film, starring Vincent Price and Tab Hunter.

Val Lewton (1904 - 1951) was a novelist, film producer, and screenwriter in Hollywood, and the original idea for *Cat People* was based on his previously published short story called *The Bagheeta* (1930), and screenwriter DeWitt Bodeen added to the script for the film adaptation. Lewton made his career by making low-budget horror classics that stand out from the regular horror genre, especially with *Cat People*, as author Grant clearly asserts, "the most highly regarded of the noir horror/dark fantasy movies Lewton produced for RKO in the 1940s" (Grant 111). The film noir style is a perfect fit for a horror thriller like *Cat People*, which is both poignant and subtle with its psychological terror, and implied violence. Lewton was born in Russia and came to the United States in 1909. From an early age Lewton was a gifted storyteller, later writing for newspapers and magazines, and by the 1930s some of his published books were being optioned for films under his pseudonyms like Cosmo Forbes and Val Lewton rather than his real name Vladimir Ivanovich Leventon.

Eventually the name Lewton stuck, his writing talent was soon spotted by legendary producer and film studio executive David O. Selznick, having used some of Lewton's well written scenes in *Gone with the Wind* (1939), while working with Selznick as a story editor, he was given the opportunity in 1942 to run the horror unit for RKO, by producing and writing extremely low-budget "B" productions. The end result made him famous and high esteem within the entertainment industry for his well-made low cost B-pictures that turned a surmountable profit every time. Lewton's career was on the rise after his successes with films like *Cat People* (1942), *I Walked With a Zombie* (1943), *The Leopard Man* (1943), *The Seventh Victim* (1943), *The Ghost Ship* (1943), *The Curse of the Cat People* (1944), *The Body Snatcher* (1945), *Isle of the Dead* (1945), and *Bedlam* (1946). He was slated to start progressing into "A" list pictures after 1946, but dealing with big budget productions and escalating health problems, forced him to make only three other films before his sudden death in 1951.

The cinematographer was Nicholas Musuraca (1892 - 1975); he began his film career in silent motion-pictures and gained experience in making B-movies for RKO in the 1930s. Musuraca often teamed up with Tourneur on several films, "he collaborated with director Jacques Tourneur on *Cat People* (1942) and *Out of the Past* (1947), (Wikipedia). Musuraca was nominated for an Academy Award for the film *I Remember Mama* (1947) and later in the 1950s started working primarily in television. "Along with Gregg Toland's work on *Citizen Kane* (1941), Musuraca's cinematography for *Stranger on the Third Floor* (1940) defined the visual conventions for the film noir and codified the RKO look for the 1940s. Musuraca's photography begins and ends with shadows, owing a major debt to German Expressionism, and can be seen as the leading factor in the resurrection of the style in Hollywood in the 1940s" (Wikipedia).

Kent Smith (1907 - 1985) plays the husband Oliver Reed in *Cat People*, Smith was an American actor with a long film career, and he first started on Broadway in 1932 in *Men Must Fight* and soon after, made his Hollywood debut in *The Garden Murder Case* (1936). Smith was known for being in leading roles primarily of "B" films and later becoming prominent as a character actor in many films and TV roles spanning over 40 years. Some of his best films include *Cat People* (1942), *Hitler's Children* (1943), *The Curse of the Cat People* (1944), *The Spiral Staircase*, (1946), *My Foolish Heart* (1949) and *The Damned Don't Cry!* (1950). Smith by the 1950s, 1960s, and through the 1970s, mainly worked in numerous television productions, on such shows like *NBC Television Opera Theatre* (1950 - 1951), *Studio One in Hollywood* (1950- 1952), *Science Fiction Theatre* (1955), *Alfred Hitchcock Presents* (1959), *The Outer Limits* (1963 -1964), *The Invaders* (1967 - 1968), and a personal favorite, the telefilm *The Night Stalker* (1972), with an assortment of talented actors like Darren McGavin, Carol Lynley, Simon Oakland, Elisha Cook Jr. and Claude Akins. Making his last appearance on TV in an episode of *Wonder Woman* (1977).

French actress Simone Simon (1910 - 2005) plays Irena Dubrovna, Simon first came to Hollywood in the 1930s, the petite former fashion designer student with striking looks, began her career in such films as *Le Chanteur inconnu* aka *The Unknown Singer* (1931) and *Girls' Dormitory* (1936). She is most prominent in the crime film noir *La Bête Humaine* (1938), also in the fantasy film, *The Devil and Daniel Webster* (1941), the atmospheric thrillers, *Cat People* (1942) and *The Curse of the Cat People* (1944). Simon didn't have a lasting film career in America, but returned to France to make more pictures there, and "she continued to appear in international productions--notably Max Ophuls's stylish erotic comedy, *La Ronde* (1950)--through the mid-1950s" (TMC), making her final screen appearance in *The Woman in Blue* (1973).

Jane Randolph plays Alice Moore in *Cat People*, the coworker and soon-to-be new love interest of Oliver Reed, even though he is married to Irena Dubrovna. Leaving her home state of Indiana, Randolph came to Hollywood in 1939 to study acting and eventually was offered small roles with Warner Bros., which later led to a contract deal with RKO giving her a leading role in *Highways by Night* (1942). From there she was cast in a variety of roles as in the atmospheric horror films *Cat People* (1942) and *The Curse of the Cat People* (1944), and playing susceptible females in film noir classics like *Jealousy* (1945) and *Railroaded!* (1947), Randolph also starred in the "classic comedy thriller *Abbott and Costello Meet Frankenstein* (1948). A year later she married sometime producer Jaime del Amo and retired to Spain and the life of a socialite. In later years she returned to Los Angeles, but also maintained a home in Switzerland" (imdb).

Tom Conway (1904-1967), who portrays Dr. Louis Judd and "was the older brother of George Sanders and shared his mellifluous speaking voice. Born in Russia to English parents, the family moved back to England when the 1917 revolution broke out. Conway had a long and wonderful career in film, playing *The Falcon* in ten films and appearing in three classic Val Lewton chillers: *Cat People* (1942), *The Seventh Victim* (1943) and *I Walked With a Zombie* (1943)" (Barebonesez). Conway appeared in several films, television, and radio programs, even "playing Sherlock Holmes following Basil Rathbone after the 1946 - 1947 radio series. In 1951, Conway replaced Vincent Price as the star of the radio mystery series *The Saint*, coincidentally taking on a role that his brother, Sanders, had played on film a decade earlier" (TCM). Conway used his talented voice as the narrator for Disney in the animation feature, *Peter Pan* (1953). In the 1950s, Conway made three episodes of *Alfred Hitchcock Presents*, he received critical praise for *The Glass Eye* (1957), the role of ventriloquist

Film Noir: The Best of The Classics

Max Collodi in a twisted tale about "true identity" (guess who the dummy really is?) and the price of being too shallow by the woman, Julia (Jessica Tandy), who falls in love with him, this particular episode is noteworthy for it was "awarded the Emmy for Best Direction for a Television Series (in 1958), this was the only Emmy won by a single episode of the *Alfred Hitchcock Presents/Hour* series in its ten-year run" (Barebonesez).

For my final thoughts, I did enjoy *Cat People* very much, and definitely rank it up there as a classic horror film noir that uses fear of the unknown, primarily as a terror factor, for what you don't see can be just as terrifying as what you can see. Looking back on the year in which the film was produced (1942) is not only nostalgic to watch, but is also the year America goes to war, and enters into unknown horrors and uncertainty during that time. I've seen *Cat People* before as a kid watching old horror films and it always reminded me of another version of the werewolf curse. As an adult, I see it now through older eyes, and admire the craftsmanship of making the film, and realized with no budget for special effects, no panther transforming makeup like Lon Chaney, Jr. had for his werewolf, limited running time, and keeping the violence down to the imagination, really works well. I do, however, question the behavior of the husband in the film, who is so quick to disregard his troubled wife, and instantly and quite openly falls into the arms of another woman.

I'm most impressed with producer Val Lewton; he was the driving force behind RKO's horror "B" films at that time, and a gifted writer. I'm sad to discover he died so young, just as his career was taking off again in Hollywood. He had to take pre-named RKO titles and create a film out of that limitation. He did an excellent job at combining metaphors into a story length movie with film noir elements. I also really appreciate a good backstory or ancient lore that comes with a horror that spans the ages, like the story of King John, who came to Irena's Serbian village to rid it of wickedness and evil, which to me adds a brief historical account of legitimacy to the curse.

Lastly, I greatly enjoyed the atmospheric setting of the exteriors (the raining night, sinister vacant streets, and eerie fog) and interiors (Irena's vast apartment, staircase, candlelight, fireplace, and Oliver's office), that will be eventually encased in obscure lighting, and evoke a familiar appeal at first and than a dreadful foreboding. Just like Irena's demeanor, she is very demure, polite, and attractive, a regular-looking young women, but with a hint of a subtle evilness about her that no one knows about or can even fathom. *Cat People* is creepy and entertaining, even today as horror films go, with no need for gory exploitation or buckets of blood. *Cat People* is a haunting, psychological tale, with elements that truly provoke the mind, and root in our deepest fears. Consider a cult classic, it is worth watching for mixing horror and film noir superbly, and a testament to showcasing what can be done with creativity on a small budget.

3

DOUBLE INDEMNITY

The film *Double Indemnity* (1944) opens up at night with Walter Niff (Fred MacMurray) an insurance salesman in 1938 is dictating a confession of murder. Told in flashbacks we see him meet an attractive married woman, Phyllis Dietrichson (Barbara Stanwyck), Niff is there to update their insurance policy, but instead plot together to kill her husband and swindle the insurance claim for $100,000 by evoking a double indemnity clause. Orchestrated by Niff who considers this a challenge to beat the system and assisted by Mrs. Dietrichson who is motivated by obtaining instant wealth, the murder must look like an accident from falling off a train. The plan works, but Niff's boss, Barton Keyes (Edward G. Robinson) isn't so sure about the so-called one-in-a-billion chances of falling off a train occurring right after acquiring the insurance policy. He immediately suspects that Phyllis has killed her husband with the help of another man, and begins to build a case around her and her unknown accomplice.

Niff realizes that his best friend Keyes is eventually going to discover the truth about Phyllis and distance himself from her. Worried about the change of events and getting caught, Niff starts investigating on his own concerning Phyllis' background. He befriends Phyllis' step-daughter, Lola Dietrichson (Jean Heather) and learns a terrible truth that she has killed before. He also stumbles on the fact that Phyllis is secretly seeing another guy and never did love him in the first place. He realizes he has been duped by Phyllis, manipulated all the way and by his own lust for her. Niff decides to take matters into his own hands by confronting her one last time to rectify the murders of Lola Dietrichson's parents. Only this time Phyllis is ready to sever their relationship permanently.

The setting for *Double Indemnity* (1944) is Los Angles and filmed in shadowy interiors and ambiguous exteriors giving way to a more imaginative, dark location that coincides with the bleakness of the characters and their story. The film goes for some realism as detailed in *The Dark Side of the Screen: Film Noir* by Foster Hirsch, "There are vestiges throughout of the real Los Angeles, of actual streets and houses rather than studio-created replicas" (Hirsch 5). This approach makes for authenticity and shows us that this could happen in a real place at any time, where the unlawful, unsatisfied, and unethical meet in the shadows to barter and make deals involving someone's murder. The principle elements that make a great film noir are encapsulated in movies the were being made in the mid 1940s, as Hirsch summarizes, "In character types, mood, themes, and visual composition, *Double Indemnity* and *Scarlet Street* offer a lexicon of noir stylistics. Set in cities at night, the two films dramatize the fateful consequences of an obsession" (Hirsch 8).

What further influenced the film noir genre was the national growing tension caused by the war. Since 1942 American life had been greatly impacted by the start of World War II, the Depression was over, the high demands for the war effort to increase production actually benefited the economy, and the United States experienced a fundamental shift in attitude. Americans were now in the business of killing and making war against Germany, Italy, and Japan (Axis powers). True, the hard times of the 1930s had ended, but the memory of criminal mayhem and economic struggle still lingered with the American psyche. The seriousness of making weapons of war and watching young men go to die in a war for freedom left an indelible mark in society and some of which translated to film.

The film is based on the James M. Cain's crime/thriller novel *Double Indemnity* published in 1936 and Raymond Chandler wrote the screenplay that was nominated for an Oscar. The film *Double Indemnity* garnished other Oscar nominations for Best Picture, Best Director (Billy Wilder), and Best Actress (Barbara Stanwyck). Cain had gained fame in 1934 with his popular novel *The Postman Always Rings Twice*, and tried to get Hollywood interested in making *Double Indemnity*, but it couldn't pass the Hays Codes, not until Billy Wilder's produced a tone down treatment and hiring Raymond Chandler to craft a skillful screenplay that pleased everyone.

Billy Wilder directed *Double Indemnity* in a controlled purposeful manner, the audience is merely an observer through the camera lens, eavesdropping on two despicable people plotting murder, as noted by Hirsch, "There seems to be no world outside the frame, and there are almost no other people on view besides the principals" (Hirsch 6). And this gives us an intimacy in their corruptive lives and mindset as we watch them fall victim to their own obsessions and greed. Wilder, a talented film director of German and French films had immigrated to the United States in the 1930s when Hitler seized power in Germany. In his long outstanding career in Hollywood he would eventually earn 6 Oscars and be nominated for 20, including Best Director for *The Lost Weekend* (1945).

John F. Seitz was the cinematographer for *Double Indemnity,* a veteran director of photography who had a long career in silent motion pictures and later in talkies. Between Wilder and Seitz they both contributed to the overall look of the film and giving it a stylistic mixture of light and shadow derived from German expressionism that was dominant in the 1920s. Now common shots and techniques associated with film noir is noted by Andre Spicer and Helen Hanson in their book *A Companion to Film Noir*, giving details such as having "heavy emphasis on subjective experience augmented by first-person point-of-view, voice-over, and flashbacks (Spicer, Hanson 52).

The mood of *Double Indemnity* is captured on a play in lighting as mentioned by Hirsch, "The film is designed as a series of visual contrasts between night and day, shadow and light. The opening scene, Walter's car is racing unsteadily through the nighttime city, is followed by a flashback set on a sunny afternoon in a Spanish-style house in Pasadena" (Hirsch 5). A film noir trait is utilizing the props or scenery to add to the shot's premise like rain, furniture, catastrophic walls, and dimness of light, as mentioned by Hirsch, "Venetian blinds break up the flow of the streaming sunlight casting ominous barred shadows onto the walls (Hirsch 5).

Walter Niff seems like your average insurance agent going about his daily routine, but leading a boring life until he falls under the alluring spell of Phyllis Dietrichson, as Hirsch observed, "suggest that the obsessiveness, the irrationality, the violence, the wrenching psychological shifts triggered by their infatuation with luscious, deceitful women were lying in wait beneath the characters' bland mask" (Hirsch 2). This fatal attraction would lead Niff down a dark slippery path he could not turn back from and he was plagued with a guilty conscious that needed somehow to rectify the murder of Mr. Dietrichson.

Phyllis Dietrichson, a former nurse to Mr. Dietrichson's first wife who ended up dying suddenly, and step-mother to Lola Dietrichson, is motivated by classic film noir themes of money and not love as Hirsch noted, "Sex is only a means to an end. The end is money" (Hirsch 3). Phyllis uses her body like a weapon to obtain what she wants from men that are susceptible to her false charms. Her apparent greed and apathy toward others shows a self-center determined woman who is willing to kill to get what she wants, money and freedom. Meeting Walter Niff was fortuitous, as Hirsch explains, "Phyllis makes a career of murdering people who get in her way. She killed her husband's first wife, she meets Walter, she wants to kill her husband, and when Walter becomes a possible threat to her, she tries to kill him too" (Hirsch 4). Phyllis is an opportunist, achieving her goals diabolically through any means possible.

Barton Keyes, insurance investigator, is Niff's boss and his motivation is strictly seeking the truth and sniffing out insurance fraud. He is the one searching for clues in the murder case of Mr. Dietrichson sudden demise. Keyes is an old hand at reading people, and not trusting people is in his blood, especially when there is a great deal of money involved. He is the unseen hero of the picture, and has to bare witness to seeing a friend fall from grace when that friend breaks from normal behavior and succumb to the whims of a deadly temptress, and his own frailties.

A tragic tale of fantasy, sex, and greed between two people who hardly like each other, but are both seeking the same thing, a chance to breakout from their mundane lifestyle and make it big somehow by planning the perfect murder with the incentive of gaining $100,000 in the process. But this particular film has already shown us the outcome from the very beginning as mentioned by authors Spicer and Hanson, "The opening sequences of *Double Indemnity* and *D.O.A.*, where a dying man enters anonymous, eerily depopulated off building at night, are also emblematic in evoking a discord between the extreme condition of the characters and the mundane spaces they occupy" (Spicer, Hanson 57).

During the onset of watching the film and getting to know the players, we learned simple facts that these are ordinary people, not harden criminals, an insurance man who is quite typical and attractive young women married to a much older man, but soon we realize that both of these average citizens have crossed the line and dipped into their most hidden desires. It is easy not to like these two characters as they plot to carry out the act of murder to gain wealth, but it is compelling enough to see how their true feelings of distain for each other is slowly revealed, and how their plan is doomed to failure from the start. In classic film noir style there isn't much of a happy ending for our two protagonists on the wrong side of the law, and found myself rooting for Edward G. Robinson's character to neatly fit the missing pieces together and ferret out the murders in due course. In conclusion, I think it was an excellent film in the story, stylistic look, and superb acting by all.

4

DETOUR

The backdrop for *Detour* (1945) is hauntingly dark and moody, plays no sympathy whatsoever for the male protagonist or for the femme fatale that taunts him. These two characters have no redeeming qualities, the man is weak-minded and the woman is cleverly evil, both have made terrible decisions in their lives, and it seems that fate has dealt them a bad hand all around. The film *Detour* begins on a long desert highway where bum-like hitchhiker Al Roberts (Tom Neal) is trying to get as far away from California as possible. Al is overwhelmed by dread of memories he wishes he could forget. A song playing in a Nevada dinner awakens past memories of himself and his girlfriend working in a New York nightclub. This flashback illustrates his life before all of this as a pianist and is narrated by Al's own voice throughout the whole movie. He tells of how he used to walk his girlfriend Sue Harvey (Claudia Drake) home in the extremely foggy streets of New York, where one night she expressed her reluctance to marriage and that she is leaving for Hollywood to find her big break to stardom.

After she departs for California, Al is left brooding over her absence, calls and informs her that he'll join her there shortly to make a new life with her there in LA. This is a one-way ticket for Al; he plans to make the arduous journey with no real money for transportation, and simply the clothes on his back. On his way to the west coast, Al is given a ride in a convertible driven by Charles Haskell (Edmund MacDonald) in Arizona. Haskell is a bookie planning to make a big score in LA and tells Al his own escapades of the past, including getting seriously scratched by a crazy lady hitchhiker. During a heavy rain storm, Al is driving at night while Haskell is asleep; he pulls to the side of the road in an attempt to pull over the convertible top. He quickly discovers that Haskell had died of a heart attack, but pulling on the side door drops the body hard onto a rock. Al panics, the police will never believe his story of how Haskell really died.

Film Noir: The Best of The Classics

Al ditched the body in the desert and assumes the identity of the dead man. Al is convinced this is his only way to save himself by taking everything the deceased man owned. Later, at a motel Al has a nightmare of the whole incident. His troubles only get worse when he meets Vera (Ann Savage), an alley cat with fatal beauty more deadly then a rattlesnake and offers her a ride to LA. During the ride their light conversation takes a bad turn as Vera snaps that she knows what Al did, that he someone killed Haskell, taken his car, clothes, money, and identity. She venomously demands all of Haskell's money and threatens to hand Al over to the police for murder. Fate has played Al with a lady that likes to inflict pain to other people before they do that to her. Her level of extortion does not end with Al, by the time they get to Hollywood, Vera has already come up with a diabolical plan to fool Charles Haskell's ailing rich father by having Al impersonate his dead son to obtain a fortune in inheritance. But Al refuses to go along with the scheme.

Al is trapped by his own weaknesses and unwillingness to simply leave, seeing himself as a victim of circumstances and by Vera's own vindictive nature to control him. They rent an apartment in Hollywood together, where the vile Vera gets drunk and threatens to call the police on Al if he doesn't start acting nice to her and do what she says. He fights back and they argue at length, she flees to the bedroom with the telephone, and locks the door. Vera shouts she going to call the police on him and she drunkenly falls onto the bed tangled up in the telephone cord. Racked by fear, Al desperately pulls hard on the telephone cord from the other room in an effort to break the line completely. Finally, he forces his way into Vera's bedroom, only to find her strangled to death by his pulling of the phone cord. His entire life is ruined by this new act of murder and his dream-life with Sue is over. Al flees out of town, heading eastward, hitchhiking back to New York. Fate lets Al make it as far as Nevada, where eventually the Highway Patrol picks him up.

T.S.Garp

The film *Detour* was adapted from Martin Goldsmith's original 1939 novel called *Detour: An Extraordinary Tale* and later he wrote the screenplay with Martin Mooney. Watching the film throughout and seeing the ultimate fate of the characters in the story, laced with surprises, shock value, and bad luck make this a truly an extraordinary tale to witness. The film *Detour* is a classic fatalistic crime story emulated rather crudely by the actors and low-budge production values. These characters fit perfectly in the film noir nuances and fanatical behavior as the director tries to do the book justice with very little money on hand. So keeping with character archetypes, settings, and plot, John Grant considers from his book *A Comprehensive Encyclopedia of Film Noir: The Essential Reference Guide,* "Much has been written psychoanalyzing *Detour,* but by all contemporary accounts the intent of he moviemakers was simply to tell a tale" (Grant 180).

This crime thriller is directed by Edgar G. Ulmer and made by the Producers Releasing Corporation, a lesser known Hollywood film studio that was part of Poverty Row, a term used for the numerous small B-movie studios of that era. PRC was only in operation between 1939 - 1947. Ulmer's *Detour* is only 68-minutes long, shot quickly with basic camera work, and because of constraints with money and time, the film is produced in an independent style with long dolly shots, sparse sets (locations), and extreme close-ups. Despite lacking in major production values the film has gained considerable fame over the last 70 years, and decidedly has made itself an effective and disturbing addition to the film noir genre made on a shoestring budget. The United States National Film Registry by the Library of Congress has selected *Detour* for preservation in the archives as artistically noteworthy.

Edgar G. Ulmer was part of the German Expressionism, a refugee from Hitler's rise to power in Germany, he immigrated to the United States becoming a Hollywood film director. Some of his most memorable films were *The Black Cat* (1934), *Detour* (1945), and my personal favorite *The Man from Planet X* (1951) was a low-budget science-fiction film. Most of his popular movies were modish and unconventional films that have achieved cult status. The cinematographer for *Detour* was Benjamin H. Kline, a veteran of film and television since the 1920s. He even filmed some recognizable TV shows like *The Three Stooges Show* (1930s - 1940s), *Thriller* (1960s), and *The Virginian* (1966). Kline did manage to get some interesting camera work while filming *Detour*, the exchange with the motorcycle cop through the car window during the rain storm and the long dolly shot of Vera getting into the car for a ride were both prominent. The overall vision of the film cinematically, adverse camera angels, lighting, and shadows equate the film noir mystique.

The main protagonist in *Detour* is hitchhiker Al Roberts (Tom Neal) a piano player traveling from New York to LA to meet his girlfriend. The film doesn't show much backstory about their relationship except that she is leaving for Hollywood at the beginning of the movie. Feeling resentful for being left behind, Al is determined to join up with his girlfriend Sue (Claudia Drake), even if he has to hitchhike all the way with total strangers. He firmly believes that fate or some unseen power has control of his destiny whenever he runs into trouble. Al doesn't take reasonability for his own actions or able to make smart decisions that could affect his fate. Life intimates art or film noir for actor Tom Neal, as author Grant mentions, "Neal led something of a noir life, hospitalizing Franchot Tone over the affections of actress Barbara Payton and later being jailed for killing his wife" (Grant 180).

Vera (Ann Savage) is Al's notorious hitchhiker he gives a ride to, a fatal mistake that gets him deeper into more trouble by films end. He is attracted to her, but soon enough her wickedness is revealed simply by opening her foul mouth, and true intentions. She is playing on his weaknesses and knows his secret about the death of Charles Haskell (Edmund MacDonald). She marks Al as a chump and proceeds to dominate him by way of threats to the police for murdering Haskell, even though it was not Al's fault. Vera motives are greed and spitefulness toward men. Her own life has been tragic and besieged with drunkenness, poverty, shams, and lawlessness. Al is mystified by his own lack of will power to run from Vera's clutches. When Al finally does take a stand against Vera, his luck gets worst by accidentally killing her in the process. Al tries to escape this new unfortunate chain of events by leaving the state, but his freedom is short-lived. His pitiful narration says it all "Whichever way you turn, fate sticks out a foot to trip you."

In conclusion, the manner in which the film *Detour* is shot is both visually and verbally abusive to the eyes and ears, many continuity problems exist (Al is thumbing a ride on the wrong side of the road), over-bearing atmospheric treatment (the extreme fog scene), and actors seemed to be locked in one gear only. Nevertheless, the film does pack a punch, it is widely popular, and demonstrates all the film noir veracity you would expect, and done so on an extremely low-budget. This is a good example of film noir in that the main character is suddenly thrust into a paranoid world of deception, crime, and murder. The movie could of easily been made for *The Twilight Zone* (1959 - 1964) or *Alfred Hitchcock Presents* (1955 - 1962) tv episodes. Al is just an average Joe, merely looking to get someplace, but falls victim to unsavory circumstances, and he is too cowardly to get himself out of it properly. *Detour* is not an impressive film to watch (technically speaking); however, it has an uncanny ability to shock you and gives us a glimpse of one man's nightmare come true.

5

THE BIG SLEEP

In Los Angeles, Private Investigator Philip Marlowe (Humphrey Bogart) takes on a new case for General Sternwood (Charles Waldron) in Los Angeles, a wealthy old gentleman seeking to stop a man named Arthur Gwynne Geiger (Theodore Von Eltz), who is blackmailing his youngest daughter, Carmen Sternwood (Martha Vickers). General Sternwood wants Marlowe to stop Geiger from extorting his family for money. But Marlowe has inadvertently stepped into several other mysteries involving he Sternwood family, such as in the disappearance of Sean Regan, employed by General Sternwood to handle previous blackmailers, the sudden murder of Geiger in a house owned by a gangster named Eddie Mars (John Ridgely), and later the death of Owen Taylor, the Sternwood's chauffeur who wanted to marry the younger sister, and it gets even more complicated when Marlowe develops a romantic interest in the spoiled and demanding older sister, Vivian Sternwood Rutledge (Lauren Bacall).

As the mystery deepens, Marlowe is compounded by yet another blackmailer, Joe Brody (Louis Jean Heydt) who may have some of the missing answers Marlowe is looking for, but he too is swiftly murdered by Carol Lundgren (Tom Raffery). Marlowe restrains Lundgren and takes him to Geiger's house which is the focal point of the secrecy behind all the murders, and he notifies the police that the death of Geiger was by Taylor's gun that killed Geiger because of his scheme to give narcotics and take photographs of his girlfriend, Carmen. The police nab Lundgren for the murder of Brody. Marlowe can reason that Brody killed the Sternwood's chauffeur to retrieve the nude photos of Carmen.

Marlow investigates the connection between gangster Eddie Mars and Vivian. Afterwards, he is severely beaten by thugs that work for Mars for asking too many questions and later gains a tip from Harry Jones (Elisha Cook, Jr.). Apparently, Jones has some information to sell on what happened to Sean Regan and where Eddie Mars's wife is and wants $200 for it. His partner Agnes Lowzier (Sonia Darrin) has all the details, she was involved with Brody in the blackmail plan, and now that he's dead, she wants to leave town for good, and needs money. Jones is bumped off (poisoned) by another of Mars' henchmen, Marlowe meets with Lowzier, pays her the $200, and she tells him where Mars's wife is hiding out. Marlowe goes there and is captured by more of Mars' thugs; knocked unconscious, he awakens in a house where he finally meets Mona Mars (Peggy Knudsen) and surprisingly Vivian.

Marlowe knows the hoods will be back soon to kill him, Vivian, now deeply in love with Marlowe unties his bounds, and helps him to escape. Canino (Bob Steele) the man that murdered Jones and Mars' other hired thug, mechanic Art Huck (Trevor Bardette), return to the house to kill Marlowe. During the climatic gunfight Marlowe kills Canino, together, he and Vivian arrive at Geiger's house, Marlowe has a plan to, and he calls Mars to let him know his boys failed, and will meet him at Geiger's house. They lay in wait to trap Mars as he comes in, Mars shows up with several more men to cover the front and back of the house in hopes of killing Marlowe as he arrives at the house. Once Mars is inside the house, Marlowe points his gun at him, demanding the whole truth regarding the Sternwood family and who really killed Sean Regan. Mars confesses that Carmen Sternwood in an intoxicated state murdered Regan when he rejected her advances and Mars used that information to extort money from General Sternwood and a hold on Vivian.

Completely satisfied, Marlowe forced Mars to walk out the front door, knowing full well the house was covered by his gang of thugs. But the foggy night prevented them from seeing clearly who left the house; Mars is mowed down by his own men in a hail of bullets. Marlowe calls the police informing them of Eddie Mars' sudden death, he omits the fact that Carmen was involved in Regan's death, but instead blames Mars for his murder. He explains to Vivian that her sister Carmen needs to be quietly committed to a mental in institution to get help, and in not so many words conveys the fact that Vivian has nothing to worry about with the police, because he loves her, and they were destined to be together.

The setting for the film *The Big Sleep* (1946) is Los Angeles in the 1930s based on the novel by Chandler, "the period of the Great Depression, when America was, as a whole, disillusioned and cynical about its prospects for the future" (Sparknotes, Themes, Motifs, and Symbols). Americans were still suffering from the bad economy and the issue of money became very important one that the author wanted to convey, "Chandler mentions money throughout the novel as an ideal, a goal for the seedy crime ring that lives within the novel. Many of the characters kill and bribe for money" (Sparknotes, Themes, Motifs, and Symbols). This is a sobering reminder to post-war Americans recovering from the disorder and lack of money of the 1930s topsy-turvy economy, "many of the characters find themselves in troublesome situations, such as Agnes Lozelle and Harry Jones, therefore mirroring the desperation in which Americans found themselves throughout the period about which Chandler is writing" (Sparknotes, Themes, Motifs, and Symbols).

The movie *The Big Sleep* is a great tale and produced in classic film noir style that is full of twist and trickery as crime stories go, and the lead character shares a kinship to the anti-hero detective Sam Spade featured in *The Maltese Falcon* (1941) five years earlier, not just because it was played by the same actor, but because the character of Philip Marlowe personifies the key elements that make a great modern-day detective. Marlowe is pessimistic, cool under pressure, cautious, clever, witty, and still fits in the genre's typical mold of a cynical detective. He is honest by profession and still a rebel, tiptoeing his way through the legal system, protecting his client and himself whenever possible.

The film *The Big Sleep* is based on a Raymond Chandler novel. The highly acclaimed crime thriller novel that Chandler wrote was popular despite possessing a convoluted storyline, but nevertheless crafted a suspenseful, moody, and intriguing book. "He wrote his first novel, *The Big Sleep*, in 1939, in a time frame of only three months. In creating the novel, Chandler cannibalized two of his earlier short stories, *Killer in the Rain* and *The Curtain*." (Sparknotes, Context). A few crime writers of that bygone era were carving out their own niche of work that would be translated into film noir and perpetuate the genre. Dashiell Hammett author of such famous books like *The Maltese Falcon* and *The Thin Man* along with Chandler's *The Big Sleep* and *Farewell, My Lovely* are both writers who got their start publishing with the celebrated crime and mystery *Black Mask* pulp magazine that operated in the 1920s to the1950s giving Hollywood amble substance to feed the film noir genre, as Foster Hirsch observed in his book *The Dark Side of the Screen: Film Noir*, the need for a new type of hero, "The typical Hemingway hero held on to his stance of self-reliant masculinities in a way that paralleled the hard-boiled starts -- the Sam Spades and Philip Marlowes -- of the *Black Mask* brigade" (Hirsch 28).

When Chandler lost his job in the oil business in the 1930s, he later turned to pursue a career as a writer and begun writing for pulp magazines. He studied hard to duplicate the crime stories he enjoyed reading and was soon ready to make his own debut novel of that genre. "The publication of *The Big Sleep*, then, came during the heart of the Great Depression and just before the start of World War II. Therefore, the novel, not surprisingly, carries with it much of the cynicism of 1930s America. The catchy dialogue of the main character, Philip Marlowe, is the epitome of what came to be known as "hard-boiled" style—the racy, clever, tough street talk of the detective narrative." (Sparknotes, Context).

This superb crime thriller is directed by Howard Hawks (1896 - 1977) and released by Warner Bros. in 1946 even though it was shot and finished in 1945, the studio sat on the film for recuts and pick-up shots, and playing off on the wonderful Bogart-Bacall chemistry. Hawks was has become legendary as a Hollywood film

Film Noir: The Best of The Classics

Director, Producer, and Writer with his signature cinematic style that goes all the way back to the 1920s to the 1970s. As mention by imdb, "Hawks made a name for himself by directing eight silent films in the 1920s, His facility for language helped him to thrive with the dawn of talking pictures, and he really established himself with his first talkie in 1930" (imdb, Howard Hawks).

Hawks could make his distinctive mark on any genre and can be easily recognized throughout his long film career, "westerns, musicals, screwball comedies, war pictures, historical epics, romantic adventures, films noir, gangster sagas, and even science fiction"(imdb, Howard Hawks). Here is just sample of classic films he has directed, *Scarface* (1932), *Bringing Up Baby* (1938), *His Girl Friday* (1940), *Sergeant York* (1941), *Air Force* (1943), *To Have and Have Not* (1944), *The Big Sleep* (1946), and *Rio Bravo* (1959). He nearly won the Oscar in 1941 for Best Director of *Sergeant York*; Hawks was "nominated for Best Director only that one time, despite making some of the best films in the Hollywood canon" (imdb, Howard Hawks). By the 1960s and 1970s the French critics were quite impressed and more thoughtful of Hawks lifetime film work, and they rallied to his defense, ultimately in 1974 Hawks was given an honorary Academy Award, "it was to the Academy's credit that it recognized the great Hawks in his lifetime. (imdb, Howard Hawks).

Hawks initially had a difficult time trying to unravel the complex storyline of *The Big Sleep*. John Grant mentions how intricate the tricky plot of *The Big Sleep* is in his book *A Comprehensive Encyclopedia of Film Noir: The Essential Reference Guide,* "a plot that's not only too complex to follow but actually, on analysis, nonsensical" (Grant 67). Hawks had quite a time trying to formulate a clear version of the script with so many plot twists, multiple characters, their motives, and ultimate final ending of the film as Grant notes, "the ambiguity was to placate the Hays Office" (Grant 67). Hawks discovered a few loose ends within the plot that didn't make sense, as Grant points out, "while working through the screenplay, Hawks and screenwriter William

Faulkner realized they didn't know who had killed the Sternwood's chauffeur, or why. Checking with the novel left them no wiser. So they asked Chandler. After awhile, he admitted he didn't know either" (Grant 67). Warner Bros. had prescreen the original *The Big Sleep* to test audiences in 1945, "unsatisfied with the original ending of the film and in conflict with the Hays Office with scenes too harsh or unseemly, another screenwriter was brought in to help; Jules Furthman, called in to do final polishing of the screenplay to effect the change" (Grant 67).

Howard Hawks was a writer too, and he surrounded himself with a team of writers he knew were talented and could produce monumental scripts. "Hawks was lucky to have worked with some of the best writers in the business, including his friend and fellow aviator William Faulkner. Screenwriters he collaborated with on his films included Leigh Brackett, Ben Hecht, John Huston and Billy Wilder" (imdb, Howard Hawks) Although all the writers mentioned are excellent and famous in their own right, I take special interest in writer Leigh Brackett, while in High School I read a great deal of science fiction novels, and enjoyed many of her books like *The Best of Leigh Brackett*, *The Sword of Rhiannon*, and *Eric John Stark: Outlaw of Mars*. Brackett was known since the 1940s to the1970s as The Queen of Space Opera, having written for many years with pulp science fiction magazines like *Planet Stories*, *Startling Stories*, and *Astounding Stories*.

Brackett was good at characterization and her long career as a top screenwriter also helped define the genre she wrote for with such classics as *The Big Sleep* (1946), *Rio Bravo* (1959), *Hatari!* (1962), *El Dorado* (1966), and *The Long Goodbye* (1973). Director Howard Hawks often teamed up with Brackett on several films and she was sought after by George Locus to help write the first sequel to Star Wars. "A noted science-fiction/fantasy author who was prolific in SF and other pulps in the 1940s; a mentor and sometime collaborator of Ray Bradbury. Died of cancer after writing the first version of the script of Star Wars: Episode V - The Empire Strikes Back (1980)" (imdb, Leigh Brackett). Above all

Film Noir: The Best of The Classics

what mattered to Hawks the most was the interaction between characters and the look of the films that audiences would remember and enjoy memorable performances. As mentioned by imdb, "Hawks came to believe that a good film consisted of at least three good scenes and no bad ones--at least not a scene that could irritate and alienate the audience. He said, "As long as you make good scenes you have a good picture--it doesn't matter if it isn't much of a story." (imdb, Howard Hawks).

Sid Hickox was the cinematography for *The Big Sleep*. "Hickox was best known as an action photographer, who excelled shooting the gritty, moody crime films and melodramas, in which Warners tended to corner the market. He collaborated particularly well with another action specialist, the director Raoul Walsh. Hickox had the uncanny ability to make productions, shot on a modest budget, look a lot classier. His best films cover the period from 1942 to 1954. They include the boxing drama *Gentleman Jim* (1942); the films noir *To Have and Have Not* (1944), *The Big Sleep* (1946), *Dark Passage* (1947) and *White Heat* (1949); and, finally, the sci-fi cult classic *Them!* (1954)" (imdb-I.S.Mowis).

The central characters in *The Big Sleep* are Philip Marlowe, P.I. (Humphrey Bogart) in LA to meet his new client, General Sternwood (Charles Waldron), and meets Carmen Sternwood (Martha Vickers), the rambunctious younger sister of Vivian Sternwood Rutledge (Lauren Bacall), Vivian later falls for the cynical P.I. as he tries to piece together the truth in a maze filled with deceit, gangsters, and killers. Bogart had risen to leading man status after his excellent performance in *The Maltese Falcon* (1941) and Casablanca (1942). Lauren Bacall rose to instant stardom starring with Bogart in *To Have and Have Not* (1944) based on the Ernest Hemingway novel. Though she was barely 20, Bacall graced the screen with astonishing sensuality and her performance became a symbol of aggressive and assertive women of that period. It became very clear to Warner Bros. studio to exploit the romantic connection both Bogart and Bacall had onscreen, and to team up with Howard Hawks again.

Marlowe the cynical PI and Vivian the confident divorcee make a great combination, these two tough characters become lovers and unlikely partners while surrounded by innuendo, blackmailers, and killers. Before this film women were viewed as a threat and deadly to unsuspecting men entangled by their hidden motives and evil natures as mentioned by Hirsch, "The anti-woman bias that runs through American films reaches an apotheosis in noir, where beautiful spider women proliferate. There are other kinds of women in the films -- me meek wives infected with a fuddy-duddy morality, strong women like Lauren Bacall, who achieve something of a parity with the men they fall for" (Hirsch 20). Marlowe and Mrs. Rutledge are one equal ground and both need each other in some capacity in order to survive the mayhem encircling them.

In closing, *The Big Sleep* is an excellent movie with suspense, screams, intrigue, gunshots, murder mystery, lies, cover-up, gang of killers, and even romance, with atmospheric rain and thunder as our intrepid detective tries to unravel the puzzling clues he discovers mostly at night as he encounters numerous suspects along the way, making this a top rated film noir genre that keeps you on the edge of your seat as you watch Marlowe try to piece it all together and at the same time avoids getting killed himself in the process. There had always been rumors about an original version of *The Big Sleep* that was thought to be lost over time, but "in 1997 there was discovered in the UCLA Film and Television Archives a pre-release cut that had been issued for the entertainment of the armed forces; it differs in several scenes from the final version. This inspired the National Film Preservation Board to add the movie to the National Registry" (Grant 67). This is a great film on many levels with great performances by the entire cast, a must see for classic film noir fans, and to watch Bogart and Bacall in their prime is worth another view.

6

OUT OF THE PAST

The film *Out of the Past* (1947) begins in a rural setting. I particularity like the opening shot, a vast scenic view of high mountains and beautiful forest. The camera presents us with a crisscross road sign showing direction, miles, to all the major cities nearby. The sign in part tells us you are entering Bridgeport and that Los Angles is 349 miles distance. A man driving a convertible enters the sleepy little town of Bridgeport. Filmed in POV of an invisible passenger riding in the back, the mysterious drive's backside is to the camera preventing us from seeing who it is as he deliberately drives up to a gas station named Jeff Bailey's. The stranger is looking for Bailey, heads over to the local café, and starts asking questions about him. And thus, begins Jeff's dilemma.

Jeff Bailey (Robert Mitchum) appears to be just a small-town owner of a local gas station in Bridgeport. But his life and that of his girlfriend Ann Miller (Virginia Huston), is shattered by the arrival of a stranger called Joe Stephanos (Paul Valentine), who recognizes Jeff, and tells him his former boss, a racketeer named Whit Sterling (Kirk Douglas) wants to see him at his place in Lake Tahoe, Nevada. Jeff has no choice, he has to go, but before he leaves, he confesses to Ann about his shady past. His real name used to be Jeff Markham, former PI, who got mixed up the wrong type of people, and a fatal attraction with a woman named Kathie (Jane Greer). Told in flashbacks to New York, where Jeff is hired by Whit to locate his missing $40,000 and his disobedient girlfriend, Kathie who took it. The trail leads him all the way to Mexico, where he finds the alluring and seductively-dressed Kathie, Jeff is instantly infatuated with her, against his better judgment.

Jeff is lured by Kathie's charms and claims of innocence. Jeff begins a romantic relationship with her and they run off together, avoiding Whit and his thugs. They begin a new life in San

Francisco when one day they are spotted by Jeff's old partner, Jack Fisher (Steve Brodie), another detective, who is incidentally now working for Whit. Fisher warns Jeff that she is a liar and a thief, nearly killing Whit for the $40,000. Fisher offers Jeff and Kathie a chance to pay him off so he doesn't inform Whit of their whereabouts, but they refuse, and Fisher and Jeff go to blows. Clearly, Jeff does not want to hurt Fisher, but Kathie kills him anyway with a handy gun she had. Perplexed by Kathie's actions and her sudden disappearance, he locates her savings account book, and sees the deposited $40,000 she had stolen from Whit!

End of long flashback, Jeff says goodbye to Ann, and knows he'll never have any peace until he goes settle a score with Whit. Upon arrival, Whit tells Jeff he has another job for him to do in San Francisco, he reluctantly agrees, and discovers that Kathie is back together with Whit. Jeff smells a rat and knows by instinct that he is being played. The job is an obvious frame-up to knock off a victim and blame it on Jeff. He even warns the victim, but it is too late, so Jeff hides the body, gumming up the works while he tries to fix things. He secretly confronts Kathie, who is obviously playing on both sides, but Jeff sees right through her lies, and discovers incriminating evidence linking him to Fisher's murder supplied by Kathie's written statement. Jeff steals the IRS files that Whit wanted, keeps them safe, and makes a deal with Whit's associates, they get the files, and dead man's body and no police, and Jeff gets the signed affidavit accusing him of murder.

The deal is set, but the police show up suddenly to claim the body, and Jeff leaves town. He runs back to Bridgeport to see Ann, police are looking for him thinking he killed two people, and he has very little time left. Caught in a web of elaborate betrayals, Jeff hides out in mountainous terrain, waiting for word of Whit. Kathie persuades Joe to follow Jeff's pal, the deaf and mute "Kid" (Dickie Moore) to where Jeff's hideout is, and kill him. But the scheme backfires, Joe falls to his death off a cliff, and Jeff heads on over to confront Kathie and Whit at his place in Lake Tahoe. Jeff lays it on the line to both Whit and Kathie by telling the whole truth, the lies of Kathie, the double-crosses, and who killed who. Whit is astounded by such betrayal by Kathie and agrees with Jeff that Kathie will take the rap for the murders, and Jeff and Whit have a deal with the missing files.

Jeff leaves and sees Ann again to remind her that whatever happens, he really does love her. When he returns to Whit's place to close the deal, he finds Whit murdered by the evil Kathie. Now he is still wanted for murder and the only man who could have saved him is lying dead on the floor. Kathie wants to run off with Jeff, stating that he can only make deals with her now, and Jeff says "You build my gallows high, baby." That says it all as Jeff realizes he has lost everything, including his dream life with Ann. He pretends to agree to go away with her and she packs her suitcase for a long trip, but Jeff has secretly phoned the police. He knows he cannot escape his dire fate and he makes damn sure that Kathie gets hers. They don't get very far, a police roadblock has been set up, and Kathie realizes that Jeff has betrayed her. She kills him and the police shoot Kathie to death, causing their car to crash.

In film noir, there is often the wrong man scenario, where the main characters are pawns and victims of criminal actions done by others, but another type of common theme is when a character's shady past comes back to haunt them, as Hirsch points out, "in *Out of the Past*, *The Killers*, *Kiss of Death*, and *The Woman on Pier 13*, characters are convicted by who they once were, in a past they have tried to overcome" (Hirsch 179). Jeff Bailey is a cynical PI spawn from the city seeking to escape its clutches. The main genesis for many film noir settings begin in the heart of the city, within the shadows, dark alleyways, around unsuspecting corners, between gorgeous lips, behind closed doors where corruption grows and sucks those in that happen to be caught by its allure of easy money and sex. "The city as a cradle of crime and a cauldron of negative energy is the inevitable setting for film noir. Country settings appear infrequently, usually as a counterpoint to the festering city" (Hirsch 83). Jeff found himself mixed up in a classic Greek tragedy and needed to leave all that he knew from the big city.

The cities in film noir are often dark, mysterious, and deadly to novice and pros alike, some people become so entangled that they are left with few options except to disappear, "leaving the contaminating city for salvation in the country is a recurrent noir pattern. Burt Lancaster in *The Killers* and Robert Mitchum in *Out of the Past* retire from lives of crime to sylvan settings. (Hirsch 83). But the escape to pleasant surroundings that are new and far away from the clutter of the crime invested city, may not be totally safe after all, as Hirsch clearly notes "a few noir movies - *They Live By Night*, *The Postman Always Rings Twice*, *Ace in the Hole*, and *Gun Crazy* - take place in rural locations" (Hirsch 83). You can take yourself out of the city jungle, but a slew of killers may come follow, bringing with them corruption, revenge, and death.

Jeff has been hiding for 3 years, he opened a modest gas station in Bridgeport, the newest addition to the peaceful town, and even starting dating a young lady, Ann. When his shady past finally catches up with him, he has to leave, but first he must explain the whole truth to his girlfriend. I like the intimate close-up shots between Jeff and Ann, especially riding in the car, in the film they share several of these and it perfectly conveys their obvious romance and trust. Enter the flashback scene 3 years prior as Jeff tells it, now here is where the real story begins, and why he has been on the run. "dramatizing the impact of the past on present action, the format of archetypal noir thrillers like *The Killers* and *Out of the Past* recalls *Citizen Kane*, the locus classicus for many noir patterns" (Hirsch 74).

Ann sits and listens to the painful memories of Jeff's previous life as PI hired to find a lady who stole $40,000. The trail leads him to Mexico, Jeff narrates throughout the film, and the entrance of Jane Geer as Kathie is breathtaking. The movie graciously promotes Jeff and Kathie's attraction by placing them in a passionate silhouette of the night along the beach that sparks a natural romance. I really enjoy the use of silhouettes to enhance an unspoken emotion between two characters, were the action is subtle, and yet defined in that moment. Both characters seem to struggle with conflicting emotions about their growing love, but a carry on as if on a romantic holiday. Even the backdrop of a rainstorm conveys the secrecy, isolation, and passion Jeff and Kathie have for each other, but is any of it real, unbeknownst to Jeff, Kathie will ultimately ruin his life repeatedly, "the doomed ex-detective is seduced once again by the charming, wicked woman he had loved and lost, and becomes hopelessly embroiled in a maze of double - and triple-crosses" (Hirsch 74).

Light and darkness is an important part in film noir, and most enjoyable when in contrast with one another. This use of lighting gives director Jacques Tourneur and cinematographer Nicholas Musuraca, an opportunity to play with light and shadow as in one of my favorite scenes is where Jeff's old partner confronts him at the hideaway cabin Jeff and Kathie have been using, the sharp light on their faces coming from the fireplace, and the rest of the room shrouded in darkness gives a chilling aspect that something is going to happen during this unexpected visit and argument. And the outcome of which leaves Jeff with no girl and framed by her for a murder he did not commit.

The movie *Out of the Past* is based on the novel *Build My Gallows High* by Geoffrey Homes (Daniel Mainwaring). Journalist turned mystery novelist, Mainwaring used his pen name Geoffrey Homes to become a successful novelist and screenwriter. Most of the settings Homes wrote about was in California small-towns where his talents shined as he depicted realistic American culture, some of his best screenplays were *The Big Steal* (1949), *This Woman is Dangerous* (1952), *The Phenix City* (1954), and the *Invasion of the Body Snatchers* (1956). To advance himself into screenwriting full time and learn more about adapting books to screen, "Homes (aka Daniel Mainwaring) was reportedly helped in adapting his own novel to the screen by actor/screenwriter Frank Fenton and novelist James M. Cain" (Grant 485).

T.S.Garp

The director of *Out of the Past* was Jacques Tourneur (1904 – 1977), an acclaimed French director of many classic film noir and low-budget horror films like *Cat People* (1942), *I Walked with a Zombie* (1943), *Berlin Express* (1948), and one of my personal favorites *Curse of the Demon* aka *Night of the Demon* (1957). Tourneur was born in France and came to America when he was just 10 years old. Over time as he got older he slowly entered the entertainment business of Hollywood, working first in silent pictures, and by the 1930s started directing for major studios like MGM, Columbia, and RKO. His film career is over 30 years long, *War-Gods of the Deep* (1964) a science fiction tale was his last film, starring Vincent Price and Tab Hunter.

The cinematographer of *Out of the Past* was Nicholas Musuraca, began his film career in silent motion-pictures and gained experience in making B-movies for RKO in the 1930s. Musuraca had worked with Tourneur before, "he collaborated with director Jacques Tourneur on *Cat People* (1942) and *Out of the Past* (1947), (Wikipedia). Musuraca was nominated for an Academy Award for the film *I Remember Mama* (1947) and later in the 1950s started working primarily in television. "Along with Gregg Toland's work on *Citizen Kane* (1941), Musuraca's cinematography for *Stranger on the Third Floor* (1940) defined the visual conventions for the film noir and codified the RKO look for the 1940s. Musuraca's photography begins and ends with shadows, owing a major debt to German Expressionism, and can be seen as the leading factor in the resurrection of the style in Hollywood in the 1940s" (Wikipedia).

Robert Mitchum plays some of America's most endearing and disorderly characters on the big screen over his long career as an actor. What makes Mitchum even more interesting as a performer is some of his own past life exploits mirror those of his onscreen personas. Born in Bridgeport, Connecticut in 1917 as Robert Charles Durham Mitchum, he was not big on authority, dropped out of school, traveled his way across the United States, and as a teenager found himself on a Georgia chain gang, from that escapade he later became a bit of a Renaissance man, learning many trades and meeting many all types of people as a boxer, shoe salesman, bouncer, and a coal miner. Eventually, he settled down in the 1940s, got married, had a family, and moved to California, where he joined the Long Beach Theatre Guild after discovering his love of acting. His talent was obvious, he quickly rose to stardom in minor roles that led to sealing a contract with RKO.

While Mitchum was building his acting chops in the 1940s, World War II broke out, and he was drafted into the military for a short time. But Mitchum returned to acting and finally got a major break, "In 1945, he was cast as Lt. Walker in *Story of G.I. Joe* (1945) and received an Oscar nomination as Best Supporting Actor. His star ascended rapidly, and he became an icon of 1940s film noir, though equally adept at westerns and romantic dramas. His apparently lazy style and seen-it-all demeanor proved highly attractive to men and women, and by the 1950s, he was a true superstar despite a brief prison term for marijuana usage in 1949, which seemed to enhance rather than diminish his "bad boy" appeal" (imdb, bio). Nevertheless, it was Mitchum's first starring role in the film *Out of the Past* in 1947 that helped him to become a well known celebrity worldwide.

Robert Mitchum was one of several film noir actors that got their start in the genre in the 1940s, like Kirk Douglas and Burt Lancaster, who later went on to become major movie stars and leading men in their own right. Mitchum in his older years, even played Raymond Chandler's Philip Marlowe in *Farewell, My Lovely* (1975) and *The Big Sleep* (1978), both films are carried by Mitchum's excellent portrayal of hard-boiled detective Marlowe. In Mitchum's past, "his noir heyday, in *Out of the Past*, and later in *The Night of the Hunter* and *Cape Fear*, Mitchum made a powerful impact" (Hirsch 163). Mitchum's character of Jeff in *Out of the Past*, ends up like many of Douglas and Lancaster's film noir characters of this era and type, where trickery and deception is the name of the game, as mentions by Grant, "an archetypal noir movie complete with archetypal femme fatale and archetypal noir cinematography, this offers little by way of emotional relaxation as it follows Jeff's course toward a nemesis made inevitable by his love for a woman who has capitulated to the evil inside her; even after he's recognized the extent of that evil, he's still not immune to her lure" (Grant 484).

Jane Geer's Kathie plays the alluring temptress to Robert Mitchum's character Jeff Bailey, with an innocent demure quality that hides a cold, calculating mind, she is poison and lethal to any man that gets taken in by her fatal attraction, "Jane Geer's dragon lady in *Out of the Past* is charming - hence especially insidious. When she materializes, dressed in white, on the street of a lazy Mexican town, she looks like the hero's daydream come to life, decidedly not like the nemesis that she reality is" (Hirsch 157). Jane Geer (1924 - 2001) is an actress that was discovered and pursued by billionaire Howard Hughes in 1943. She was still a teenager, but very attractive having already had experience as a young model professionally and in numerous talent/beauty contests as a child. She left high school early to pursue singing and dancing when Hughes put her under contract. By 1945, Geer had left Hughes and was finally signed by RKO, where she gained leading roles in the 1940s and by 1947, landed the femme fatale in *Out of the Past*. She continued acting for many years into the 1950s, but by the 1960s slowed her acting career in favor to rise a family.

What also makes *Out of the Past* likeable is the memorable performances by rising star Kirk Douglas as the suave corrupt businessman Whit Sterling. Douglas will maker several more film noirs as heavies and later become a superstar in various and iconic roles in such movies like *20,000 Leagues Under the Sea* (1954), *Lust for Life* (1954), *Gunfight at the O.K. Corral* (1957), *Paths of Glory* (1957), *The Vikings* (1958), *Spartacus* (1960), *The List of Adrian Messenger* (1963), and *Seven Days in May* (1964).

Out of the Past is a perfect example of how a film noir could be, has all the familiar qualities of femme fatale, cynical detective, and killers, but a new twist is introduced by adding regret and double-crosses. Directed by Jacques Tourneur, an expert in German expressionism and using realism with settings and locations that improve the quality of film and propels the story. I've been a fan of Tourneur since he made the horror classic film *Cat People* and the science fiction film, the original *Invasion of the Body Snatchers*. I totally didn't realize and had never seen *Out of the Past* before this review, and had missed out on appreciating his great talent for his ability to shoot in any genre. Partnered with a solid script by Daniel Mainwaring with memorable dialogue from Jeff's character like, "You're like a leaf that the wind blows from one gutter to another. You can't help anything you do, even murder."

The casting is superb and the teaming up Robert Mitchum, Jane Geer, and Kirk Douglas is excellent. Both Mitchum and Douglas will become icons in the 1950s and 1960s, and share a unique chemistry style that many actors wished they had. At the end of the film, we're all hoping that Mitchum's character, Jeff, will get away clean with a new deal he makes with Whit, throughout the entire film Jeff has been one step ahead of the liars and killers, but Whit and Jeff are outmaneuvered by the evil Kathie, both fall victim to her ruthlessness. Kathie has led Jeff down a doomed path he can't ever escape from. I like the fact that Jeff is mostly honest and has one final plan to stop Kathie's wicked cycle of murder and blackmail. Jeff was redeemed subtly one last time again, having the forethought to let his true love, Ann off the hook, and scandal that might surely follow her. "Jeff's employee and friend, a deaf/dumb, mute known just as The Kid, conveys to Ann, as requested (it's implied) by Jeff, that at the end it was with Kathie that Jeff's allegiance lay, thereby leaving Ann free to live the rest of her life" (Grant 485). This marvelous film ends on that note, leaving us to ponder the brave, foolhardy, hard-boiled PI that met the wrong girl for all the wrong reasons, but ultimately saved the right girl for all the right reasons. "This movie was remade as *Against All Odds* (1984) and added to the National Film Registry in 1991" (Grant 485). If you are looking for a quintessential film noir, full of snappy dialogue, trench coats, cigarettes, double-crosses, femme fatale, and cynical tough-guys, than look no further, you will not be disappointed.

Film Noir: The Best of The Classics

7

THE THIRD MAN

The Third Man is a film noir mystery that exudes in a dreamlike setting, creating a world that is even more exaggerated, disturbing, and strange. The location in the film is post-war Vienna, despite having been once a beautiful, thriving city, however, in the aftermath of the war with Nazi Germany, has left it partially obliterated, with impact craters, abandon buildings, and crumbling foundation. Nevertheless, Vienna still holds its old world charms intact through its people and surviving architecture as the main character played by actor Joseph Cotten ventures onto the cobblestone streets, grand archways, traveling deeper into the city, and the mystery of who the third man was that found the body of his dead friend. This interesting backdrop isn't missed by the filmmakers, who use it in the classic film noir style by masterfully employing the use of natural symbols, light and shadows, and utilizing them, as mentioned in the Foster Hirsch's book, *The Dark Side of the Screen: Film Noir,* "symbolic use of the ordinary environments, noir also relies on surreal and exotic settings: the huge Ferris wheel in which the climactic meeting takes place between Orson Welles and Joseph Cotton" (Hirsch 86). Another excellent scene is deep underground in the gigantic and vast sewage system of Vienna.

This movie is indeed, incredibly good, it has a great murder mystery, humor, action, a cynical protagonist or out of work writer, take your pick, a twist or revelation toward the end of the film, great soundtrack, and a climax that is fulfilling. John Grant, author of *A Comprehensive Encyclopedia of Film Noir: The Essential Reference Guide* notes that "*The Third Man* ranks as #1 in the British Film Institute's list of the top 100 UK movies, and the ranking is merited; it retains the same immediacy today it had on release" (Grant 641). And decidedly so, it ranks high on film noir list, and even gains top marks for being regarded as an outstanding film in its own right, and as Hirsch points out, the film is "strongly influenced by German Expressionism, noir operates in a world of virtuoso contrasts between light and shadows" (Hirsch 106). Orson Welles is seen throughout the movie in cleverly deigned silhouettes, mostly at night, with shots of near total darkness, caught between search lights and the eerie echoes in the dark.

The film begins with the iconic image of London's Big Ben clock towering over the city. This cuts to an extreme close-up of a guitar zither playing the catchy soundtrack throughout the film. The narration is provided by director Carol Reed, who starts the tale of the film as a montage of scenic views of Vienna is shown, and as a train arrives at a station, introduces us to American writer Holly Martins (Joseph Cotten), who is described as being happy as a lark and penniless, hoping to meet up with his old friend, Harry Lime (Orson Welles), who has promised him a job. However, almost instantly he learns that his friend is dead, killed after being struck by a speeding car.

He is soon accosted by Major Calloway (Trevor Howard) and Sergeant Paine (Bernard Lee), they represent the local British army/police division of Vienna, and warn him to go back home, and forget Lime. But Martins is overly curious about the puzzling circumstance regarding his late friend's death. He meets the attractive Anna Schmidt (Alida Valli), Lime's former girlfriend, and starts inquiring about the Lime's accident to the locals, and uncovers too many unanswered questions and a gang of liars, all telling a different story about how Harry Lime died. Martins is sure about one thing, there was seen a mysterious third man carrying the body to the curve after the accident. But who was this third man? Nobody seems to know. The more Martins investigates, the more he uncovers about Harry Lime's racketeering activities, and criminal behavior.

A chance sighting of Lime on the dark streets of Vienna convinces Martins that his friend is might still be alive. But just as fast, Lime suddenly disappears from view, vanishing once again in the darkness. Or was it merely a dream? Martins finally reasons it out that Lime is indeed alive and calls out to his cohorts that he demands to see him. A secret meeting at a Ferris wheel reveals to Martins that his old friend is very much alive, but different, Lime has become obsessed with making wealth at any cost, callous, and wanted by the law. Lime has faked his own death to avoid prosecution in Europe and is hiding in Vienna.

Unable to reconcile with what his friend has become, Martins decide to help the British police to catch Lime. However, Anna Schmidt foils the plan as she is still somewhat in love with Harry Lime, by warning him before the police can grab him. In an excellent climatic scene, Lime escapes underground, being chased by an army of police beneath the dank and dark catacombs of Vienna's sewage system. Lime evades them at first, but soon is trapped, and wounded by the police. Lime has no where to run to anymore, he is nearly finished, and rather than let the police execute him or spend his life in jail, he silently motions Martins to mercifully shoot him before the police catch him. Holly Martins complies with his old friend's request. After the real funeral is over, Martins lingers on the long road for Anna Schmidt (a great long-distant shot as she walks the entire length of the road to almost a close-up), who he feels has an obvious connection with, but she walks on by, still lingering to her devotion to Harry Lime. Nevertheless, she might come around, as Holly Martins often reminded her of her missing boyfriend, so much so she called him "Harry" several times by mistake. This fact does not escape Martins, who will stay in Vienna a little longer because of her at the film's end.

Interestingly, there were two versions of the film, one of American actor Joseph Cotton as the character Holly Martins narrating at the beginning of the film and one of director Carol Reed doing the narration in his British accent. "The UK release - the version almost universally shown today - contains 11 minutes that were cut for the US release, and has voice-over narration for its prologue done by Reed rather than by Cotton" (Grant 642). I rather like the Reed narration with his precise tone and voice for the part of narration, as the film takes place in old world Europe and Vienna. As the film unfolds, it is the American that is the foreigner in a foreign land, which is divided by four zones occupied by different parties, American, British, Russian, and France. This film takes place just as the Cold War is beginning with Russia and the added murder mystery in Vienna intensifies as each sector representing different countries vie for control and any lawlessness.

Carol Reed (1906 - 1976) directed *The Third Man* in 1949, a British film director and producer best known for films such as *Odd Man Out* (1947), *The Fallen Idol* (1948) and *The Third Man* (1949), which is considered one of the best films in cinema history, ranked #73 on Sight & Sound's Critics' Top 100 Films of all time. "Every decade, the British film magazine Sight & Sound asks an international group of film professionals to vote for the greatest film of all time. The Sight & Sound accolade has come to be regarded as one of the most important of the "greatest ever film" lists. The American film critic Roger Ebert described it as "by far the most respected of the countless polls of great movies—the only one most serious movie people take seriously" (Wikipedia). Reed also directed *The Agony and the Ecstasy* (1965) and *Oliver!* (1968), in which he received the Academy Award for Best Director.

Reed started out as a theater actor the 1920s, with Edgar Wallace's troupe, and by the early 1930s, he worked as a dialogue director for Associated Talking Pictures, and quickly rose to second-unit director and an assistant director. His film career grew under the collaboration of top leading producers such as Alexander Korda, Basil Dean, J. Arthur Rank and Edward Black. Reed's directorial debut came with *Midshipman Easy* (1935) and *Laburnum Grove* (1936); both are noteworthy and mark the beginning of his venture into films adapted from books. *The Third Man* is based on author Graham Greene's novella by the same name. Two other popular films by Reed, and personal favorites, are *Trapeze* (1956) starring Burt Lancaster, Tony Curtis, and Gina

Film Noir: The Best of The Classics

Lollobrigida, and *Our Man in Havana* (1959) starring Alec Guinness, Maureen O'Hara, and Burl Ives.

Casting a huge shadow over the film's success is having Orson Welles play a part in the movie, over the years unfounded speculation rose that the iconic Welles was more secretly involved in the creation of *The Third Man*, as Grant notes, "There have been persistent rumors that somehow Welles was responsible for the movie's brilliance, reworking the screenplay and, unacknowledged, masterminding the direction - that Reed was just a puppet. These rumors are untrue" (Grant 641). Orson Wells was hardly on the film set, he was only in certain key scenes, and in mere glimpses, as he was indeed the *missing third man* in most of the film. Reed had to use his own hands in the cut-way scene where Welles is trying to gain his freedom from a sewage steal grate. Another actor almost got the part, "Robert Mitchum would have been offered the role of Harry Lime - despite Reed's own preference for Welles - had Selznick not become worried Mitchum's recent marijuana bust might deter audiences in the US Midwest" (Grant 642).

Graham Greene wrote the screenplay and novella for *The Third Man*. Greene is an acclaim English writer, whose popular literary body of work consisted of thrillers, political, and religious novels. Highly successful as an author, Greene was equally adept in writing screenplays, and most of his novels were adapted into films, as mentioned by Hirsch, "Graham Green's mysteries are filled with noir motifs in theme, characterization, setting, and mood, as suggested in this climatic scene from Green's The Third Man" (Hirsch 49). Greene's life mirrors that of Ernst Hemmingway, it is sparked with excitement and adventure, published his first work of poetry at age 21, and published his first novel by age 29, Greene was also a world traveler, and even recruited in War World II by MI6 to be a British spy. Greene's tales of escapees during his tenure as a secret agent inspired some of his novels, as it did for Ian Fleming who wrote James Bond.

"Had *The Third Man* (1949) been the only movie cinematographer Robert Krasker ever shot, it would still secure his place in the history of film. Krasker's masterful use of shadows, camera angles and close-ups perfectly reflected the pessimism and upheaval of post-war Europe. It earned him an Academy Award and continues to influence cinematographers" (TCM). Indeed, the acclaimed Australian born cinematographer as a young adult gained his artistic education in Paris and earned photography skills while studying in Germany, and finally returning to England to learn filmmaking. Not long after, Robert Krasker (1913 - 1981), by the 1930s spent much of his time moving up from camera operator to director of photography in England. Krasker was greatly influenced by German Expressionism of the 1920s and translated that to his style of film noir in the 1940s.

Carol Reed teaming up with Krasker, who was well established in the 1940s as a master of the use of light and shadow, made *The Third Man* even more spectacular with slanted camera angles and characteristic shadows among the Vienna's post-war landscape and ancient architecture. Some of Krasker's other best and most interesting films are *Henry V* (1945) starring Laurence Olivier, *Brief Encounter* (1945), *Odd Man Out* (1947), *El Cid* (1961), *The Fall of the Roman Empire* (1964), *The Collector* (1965), and *The Trap* (1966). Reed also insisted on using the talented Anton Karas to compose the Vienna theme soundtrack using a zither for *The Third Man*, which became a big hit in 1949, better known as "The Harry Lime Theme" song. Between the great collaboration of director, writer, cinematographer, and music, the film taken as a whole is stupendous and a shinning example of the art of filmmaking that stands the test of time.

The lead role of Holly Martins as the out of work American novelist (who writes pulp Westerns) is played by Joseph Cotton (1905 - 1994). Cotton is highly regarded as a stage, radio, television, and film actor. His impressive body of work spans over 40 years in the entertainment industry as he began acting in the late 1920s, mostly with the theater in New York, without much success at first, but Cotton continued in drama-related jobs, and appeared in numerous stage plays honing his craft, but it wasn't until in the 1930s that he joined up with Orson Welles that things started to turn around and take off acting-wise for Cotton. Joseph Cotton is often described as "quietly intense, highly talented member of Orson Welles' Mercury Theater, a former drama critic who went to Hollywood with the director to act (as a drama critic) in "Citizen Kane" (1941) and stayed to enjoy success on screen, TV and stage alike over the next four decades. Tall, wavy-haired and gentlemanly, with a trace of a Southern drawl and attractive if unconventional features, Cotten developed great versatility during his 1930s stage work which would serve him well in one of the most impressive strings of performances any Hollywood actor achieved in the 40s" (TCM).

Some of Cotton's best films are *Citizen Kane* (1941), *The Magnificent Ambersons* (1942), *Journey into Fear* (1943), *Shadow of a Doubt* (1943), *Love Letters* (1945), *Duel in the Sun* (1946), *Portrait of Jennie* (1948), *The Third Man* (1949), and some of his other noteworthy films are, *Othello* (1952), *Niagara* (1953), *Touch of evil*, (1958), *From the Earth to the Moon* (1958), *Hush...Hush, Sweet Charlotte* (1964), *The Abominable Dr. Phibes* (1971), *Soylent Green* (1973), *Airport '77* (1977), *Heaven's Gate* (1980), and his final film, *The Survivor* (1981).

To express the bond that Orson Welles and Joseph Cotton had as lifelong friends is best described by this account "on June 8, 1981, Cotten had a heart attack followed by a stroke that affected his speech center. He began years of therapy which in time made it possible for him to speak again. As he began to recover, he and Orson Welles talked on the phone each week for a couple of hours: "He was strong and supportive," Cotten wrote, "and whenever I used the wrong word (which was frequently) he would say, 'That's a much better word, Jo, I'm going to use it.'" He and Welles would meet for lunch and reminisce, and when Cotten said he had written a book Welles asked for the manuscript and read it that same night. In a phone conversation on October 9, 1985, Welles told his friend and mentor Roger Hill that Cotten had written a book, and Hill asked how it read. "Gentle, witty, and self-effacing, just like Jo," Welles replied. "My only complaint is that it's too brief." Welles died the following day" (Wikipedia).

The role of the mysterious Harry Lime in *The Third Man* is played Orson Welles (1915 - 1985), a character that doesn't appear in the film until nearly the end of the movie, but his sudden appearance and presence makes for a climatic final. Much as been said about Welles involvement in the making of the film, citing on the fact that he was well-known as a director, producer, writer, and actor in his own right. And the fact that he won an Academy Award eight years before for writing and Original Screenplay for *Citizen Kane,* and nominated for Best Director and Best Actor in a Leading Role for *Citizen Kane.* The versatile Welles often narrated numerous films like *The Magnificent Ambersons* (1942) and *Duel in the Sun* (1946), but he can also be seen as a confident actor in *Jane Eyre* (1943), *The Stranger* (1946), *The Lady from Shanghai* (1947), *Macbeth* (1948), *The Third Man* (1949), *Othello* (1952), *Moby Dick* (1956), *Touch of Evil* (1958), and *The Trail* (1962).

Welles had prior experience as a Broadway actor and writer, had his own radio show at The Mercury Theatre on the Air in New York in the 1930s, where he worked with Joseph Cotton, and created the effectively realistic version of H.G. Wells' *War of the Worlds* broadcast on October 30, 1938 that frightened the whole country into thinking an invasion of Martians had landed. An ambitious, daring, and sometimes underrated, Welles has been equally good at playing leading man roles and diverse smaller character roles onscreen. His portrayal of Harry Lime, the heartless, cynical racketeer, and criminal on the run from the law is spot-on.

Alida Valli (1921- 2006), plays Anna Schmidt, Harry Lime's discarded girlfriend in the film, she reluctantly helps Holly Martins in his investigation of the real cause of Lime's death and who the third man really was. Valli was an Italian actress who appeared in more than 100 films, "Enigmatic, dark-haired foreign import Alida

Film Noir: The Best of The Classics

Valli was dubbed "The Next Garbo" but didn't live up to postwar expectations despite her cool, patrician beauty, remote allure and significant talent. She studied dramatics as a teen at the Motion Picture Academy of Rome and Centro Sperimentale di Cinematografia before snaring bit roles in such films as *Three Cornered Hat* (1935) and *The Two Sergeants* (1936). She made a name for herself in Italy during WWII playing the title role in *Manon Lescaut* (1940), won a Venice Film Festival award for *Piccolo mondo antico* (1941), and was a critical sensation in *We the Living* (1942). Following her potent, award-winning work in the title role of *Eugenie Grandet* (1946), she was discovered and contracted by David O. Selznick to play the murder suspect Maddalena Paradine in Alfred Hitchcock's *The Paradine Case* (1947). She was billed during her Hollywood years simply as "Valli," and Selznick also gave her top femme female billing in Carol Reed's classic film noir *The Third Man* (1949), but for every successful film--such as the ones previously mentioned--she experienced such failures as *The Miracle of the Bells* (1948), and audiences stayed away.

In 1951 she bid farewell to Hollywood and returned to her beloved Italy. In Europe again, she was sought after by the best directors. Her countess in Luchino Visconti's *Senso* (1954) was widely heralded, and she moved easily from ingénue to vivid character roles. Later standout films encompassed costume dramas as well as shockers and had her playing everything from baronesses to grandmothers in such films as *Eyes Without a Face* (1960), *The Gigolo* (1960), *Oedipus Rex* (1967), *Tender Dracula, or Confessions of a Blood Drinker* (1974), *1900* (1976), *Suspiria* (1977), *Luna* (1979), *Inferno* (1980), *Aspern* (1982), *A Month by the Lake* (1995) and, her most recent, *Angel of Death* (2002)" (Wikipedia).

English actor, Trevor Howard (1913 - 1988), plays Major Calloway, the man that has been trying to arrest Harry Lime for his dishonest and fraudulent business dealings in Vienna for a long time. Howard has had a long film career spanning over 40 years, often cast to play military men, spies, and distinguished gentlemen. Howard, a staged trained actor gained critical acclaimed in the film *Brief Encounter* (1945), and some of his most popular film included *The Third Man* (1949), *Around the World in Eighty Days* (1956), with David Niven, *Mutiny on the Bounty* (1962), with Marlon Brando and Richard Harris, *Father Goose* (1964), with Cary Grant and Leslie Caron, *Von Ryan's Express* (1965), Frank Sinatra, *The Liquidator* (1965), Rod Taylor and Jill St. John, *Superman* (1978), with Christopher Reeve, and *Gandhi* (1982), with Ben Kingsley.

For my final thoughts, this is one of those films you really have to see to appreciate the quality of the filmmaking craft at its best. Most people assume that super-talented director-writer Orson Welles had something to do with the superb film noir qualities and story elements within the film, but Welles was just another actor in this production, and not even seen until well into the late haft of the movie. The main credit goes to director Carol Reed and cinematographer Robert Krasker, as John Grant mentions in his book about the film, "Krasker's cinematography won an Oscar and Reed took the Grand Prize of the Festival at Cannes" (Grant 641). Their filmmaking collaboration, along with a group of talented actors, and Graham Greene's writing made *The Third Man* one of the greatest films of all time. A must see.

8

GUN CRAZY

The film *Gun Crazy* gives an important example of characters being consumed by several damaging fixations, namely the allure of femme fatales and possessing a dangerous gun fetish. This film is a psychological tale, as film author Foster Hirsch notes in his book *The Dark Side of the Screen: Film Noir*, "*Gun Crazy* makes passing stabs at a variety of meaty subjects: the place of violence in American life; the link between violence and sex; the emasculating obsession with masculinity" (Hirsch 195). The crime wave of the past decades (1930s and 1940s) during which the film takes place left an indelible mark on American society, the lure of easy money by simply robbing people with using a loaded gun, and the lure of sexually charge women coupled with the excitement of the thrill of stealing to prove oneself from a passive stance to one of manliness.

Gun Crazy is an excellent B-movie, but it had a rough beginning when it was originally released in 1949 by United Artists, and as it sometimes happens during the whole process of filmmaking with pre-production and post-production, several changes can take place before a film is ultimately released nationwide, the director, producers, and editors must work meticulously to finish a product worth showing to audiences. Any last minute changes usually takes place in post-production, and might entail changing the music, adding voice-overs, narration, dubbing, recalling the principle actors for adding pickup shots (changes in costume, location, and adding new scenes), and even altering the name of the entire movie to help sell it to the masses, as John Grant mentions in his book *A Comprehensive Encyclopedia of Film Noir: The Essential Reference Guide,* "a flop on first release as *Deadly Is the Female*, this was re-release the following year (1950) under the current title and has been widely hailed as among Hollywood's very finest B-movies" (Grant 276).

T.S.Garp

The opening scene of *Gun Crazy* begins on a street corner during a heavy rainstorm, dramatic music plays loudly as a young teenager (Russ Tamblyn) approaches a hardware shop window, he is soaking wet, eyeing something he wants behind the glass. It turns out to be a gun. He breaks the window with a rock, grabs the gun, some shells, and takes off running down the street. But the heavy downpour is so bad, flooding the entire street, the young man falls into the watery street face first, and losing everything in his hands. The gun slides over to a tall man who picks it up, he looks hard at the boy, and the boy looks up at him, and he realizes that it's the local sheriff. This is how we first meet Bart Tare as a troubled teenager, and this sets the stage for a life obsessed with being "gun crazy" and a downhill spiral for the young man by his fetish for guns, and years later by the cruel manipulation of his future wife, Laurie.

After going through the court process, sent away out of town for several years, and spending some time in the military, Bart (John Dall) returns to his hometown, and while attending a carnival, he meets a woman he instantly falls in love with, Annie "Laurie" Starr (Peggy Cummins), a trick shooter that loves guns as much as he does. They soon get married and all seems fine, until Laurie starts complaining about their money problems, and comes up with an old idea she has had for a long time about making some fast income, by stealing it. Decent Bart is against it, but his wife is immoral, cunning, and claims she will leave him if he doesn't. Bart is the weakest one in their relationship, and grudgingly complies with her wishes. Thus, begins their crime spree across America, very much like Bonnie and Clyde did in the 1930s, robbing banks, hotels, stores, and stealing getaway cars, all to feed their extravagant traveling lifestyle.

Bart is averted to any killing during the robberies, but his psychotic wife has other plans (since she has killed before), and will do so again if things don't go her way. Bart is rather helpless in his love for Laurie, he tries to quit from stealing, but Laurie persuades him to do just one more job, and then promises to stop.

Film Noir: The Best of The Classics

The last job is botched by Laurie, she purposely kills two people on the way out, horrified, Bart soon realizes that his beloved wife is a bit unstable, and the police are hunting them day and night across the entire country.

They evade the police dragnet long enough to make it to Bart's hometown and seek shelter in his older sister's house. Ruby Tare Flagler (Anabel Shaw), Bart's sister knows he did not murder those people. She warns him to leave, but two childhood friends, one a policeman, know Bart and Laurie are in the house. They manage to flee from the police again and escape into the mountainous terrain and try to lose themselves in the thick forest. Bart and Laurie get trapped in a swamp filled with dense fog. As the police close in, Laurie is not going out easy; she is ready for a fight. She takes aim at two of Bart's old friends that are approaching them without any guns, they try to convince Bart to give up peacefully, but crazy Laurie is about to kill them both, Bart shoots her dead, and the police task force kills him in a hail of bullets.

Joseph H. Lewis is the director of *Gun Crazy*, a superb and adaptable director primarily of B-movies (low-budget westerns, action pictures and thrillers) with a career spanning over 30 years in Hollywood. Lewis gains his skills while working in Hollywood as a professional camera assistant in the 1920s, "and further honed them in the MGM editorial department in the early '30s. After that Lewis edited serials at Republic and served the remainder of his apprenticeship as second unit director. He was signed to a full directing contract by Universal in 1937" (imdb, bio). Lewis had the special capacity to hold his unique creative vision despite studio restrictions, "A master of expressive lighting, tight close-ups, tracking and crane shots and offbeat camera angles and perspectives, Lewis possessed an instinctive sense of visual style, which imbued even the most improbable of his B-grade westerns and crime melodramas" (imdb, bio).

Lewis' best films were *The Big Combo* and *Gun Crazy*, in the film noir variety, and display his artistic talent, "the term 'style over content' fits director Joseph H. Lewis like a glove. His ability to elevate basically mundane and mediocre low-budget material to sublime cinematic art has gained him a substantial cult following among movie buffs. The Bonnie & Clyde look-alike *Gun Crazy* (1950), shot in 30 days on a budget of $400,000, is often cited as his best film" (imdb, bio). Lewis is also remembered for making great mysteries like "*My Name Is Julia Ross* (1945) and *So Dark the Night* (1946).

Respected for his artistic efforts, Lewis had that special quality the French called auteur when making a picture truly in his vision. Lewis was a chameleon with each film he directed and still managed to input his style while maintaining the mood of the characters in the story and designing the scenery to fit the tempo of the film, as Hirsch recognizes, "Lewis shifts his own style to accommodate the style of his characters and their setting. The detective in *So Dark the Night*, on the surface, is sedate and implacable, a man of absolutely sober deportment; and the film's own measured manner echoes the character's. The fugitive couple in *Gun Crazy* have a very different rhythm. The woman, who goads the man into a life of crime, is wildly impulsive, forever on the run; to capture her essential spirit. Lewis adopts a more expansive style than the one he used fatherlier film. He gives *Gun Crazy* a nervous, jagged movement" (Hirsch 134).

The screenplay for *Gun Crazy* was by Dalton Trumbo and MacKinlay Kantor. However, if you look at the original writing credits for the film, you'll discover it says "MacKinlay Kantor and Millard Kaufman" as such at that time during the Hollywood blacklist of the 1940s and 1950s, many professional screenwriters, actors, directors, and musicians were barred from working in the entertainment industry if they were suspected of having any affiliation with the Communist Party. The blacklist was purely political and part of the Red Scare of the Cold War era that swept the nation at that time, but ultimately destroying many careers in Hollywood in the process. As Grant clarifies in his book, Trumbo managed to keep working during this harsh period, "Millard

Film Noir: The Best of The Classics

Kaufman was fronting as scripter for Dalton Trumbo, who has been blacklisted during Hollywood's McCarthyite witch hunt" (Grant 276).

The story for *Gun Crazy* is based on a short story published in *The Saturday Evening Post* and written by MacKinlay Kantor in 1940. If you look closely at the film, you can see the distinctive parallels to real world crime sprees involving delinquent couples on the run from the law, as Grant observes, "*Gun Crazy* was based very loosely on the crime career of Bonnie Parker and Clyde Burrow; among others with the same basis are *You Only Live Once* (1937) and of course *Bonnie and Clyde* (1967), (Grant 276). What makes *Gun Crazy* a step above other common B-movies is the interesting use of shooting in real-time, hand-held (or backseat shots), and POV shots throughout the film, these camera techniques are not widely used among big budget conventional studios and filmmakers, but it is highly used by lower budget and independent filmmakers of any era, and became especially synonymous during the indie film period of 1990s, with soon-to-be famous directors like Quentin Tarantino, Robert Rodriguez, and The Coen Brothers.

The cinematography for *Gun Crazy* was done by Russell Harlan, born and raised in Los Angeles, he grew up in the early 1900s as the film industry grew, and took over Hollywood. Harlan began working in Hollywood as a lab assistant at Paramount in 1924. By the 1930s, Harlan made a number of B-Westerns, gained experience making over 30 films for director Lesley Selander. Harlan was doing very impressive work and soon moved into higher-budgeted pictures. In 1944, he was picked to shoot *A Walk in the Sun* (1945) by veteran director Lewis Milestone. But Harlan's partnership with director Howard Hawks is most noteworthy, "as John Baxter wrote in his entry on the cinematographer in *International Dictionary of Films and Filmmakers*, Hawks and Harlan "created a bleak and unromantic picture of the west that had hardly been seen since the days of Thomas Ince and William S. Hart" (TMC). Hawks and Harlan complemented each other on such films as *Red River* (1948), the science fiction/horror film *The Thing* (1951), *The Big Sky* (1952), *Land of the Pharaohs* (1955), and *Rio Bravo* (1959), and Harlan did the cinematography for two of my other favorite films *Blackboard Jungle* (1955) and *To Kill a Mockingbird* (1962).

The film *Gun Crazy* is an inspiration to independent filmmakers, especially the way Harlan shot it in 1949, "what is arguably, for students of cinematography and film noir, his technical masterpiece, *Gun Crazy* (1950). The film revolved around a gun-obsessed couple (played by Peggy Cummins and John Dall) who commit robberies. A bank robbery scene, shot in real-time, is mentioned in several books on film noir. Harlan and his crew removed the back of a stretch Cadillac in order to fit a 35mm camera (much larger than today), and as the actors drove around Montrose, California, the camera filmed everything through the windshield, making it seem like a documentary. While *Gun Crazy* was not a box-office hit, Harlan's work influenced many filmmakers, including Jean-Luc Godard, when he shot *Breathless* (1960), (TMC). Russell Harlan was nominated six times for an Academy Award and in high demand all the way to his retirement in the 1970s.

The role of Barton Tare is played by American actor, John Dall, a Broadway trained actor in the 1940s, Dall gradually moved up into motion pictures and in his very first movie, he was nominated for Best Supporting Actor for his role in *The Corn Is Green* (1945). His big break occurred again just a few years later when he was cast by legendary director, Alfred Hitchcock, to play a demented killer in the film *Rope* (1948) that also starred Jimmy Stewart. Dall, two years later, would be forever remembered in the film noir *Gun Crazy*, and has since been deemed one of the best "psycho-thrillers" in the B-movies variety. Critics labeled Dall as average and not a very strong actor, but some of his best known films have gained cult statues today, even though most of them were flops at the box office when first released like *Rope* (1948),

Film Noir: The Best of The Classics

Gun Crazy (1950), *Spartacus* (1960), and *Atlantis, the Lost Continent* (1961).

To describe the toxic character of Laurie (Peggy Cummins) in *Gun Crazy*, one need not seek any further then viewing at one of the many movie posters advertising the film back in the 1950s. An example of one reads as follows, "The Flaming Life of Laurie Starr (The Lethal Blonde). Her violent loves! Her vicious crimes! Her wild escapes!" This description most accurately portrays Laurie and her life of crime, as she undertakes with her reluctant husband, Bart. As Grant states, "Cummins, although by far the lesser actress, plays her role very much in the guise of Veronica Lake, with all of the Lake mannerisms and speech patterns - even the hair. From such deceptions emerged one of noir's great classics" (Grant 276).

The Welsh-born Irish actress, Peggy Cummins, had a 20 year career in films, but she is most remembered for "her performance in Joseph H. Lewis' *Gun Crazy* (1949), playing a trigger-happy femme fatale who robs banks with her lover" (Wikipedia). While watching the film *Gun Crazy*, it is easy to point out what sets Bart down a doom path of devastation, it is his psychotic wife, and his strange devotion to her, but in actuality it is something more, a deep seeded compulsion with firearms on a subconscious level, as Grant aptly explains in his book, "while it's easy to read the sexually dominant Starr as the femme fatale of this piece, the seductress who lures nice-guy Tare into a downward spiral of moral degradation, she's a poor fit for the part. Really it's the gun, and its quasi-sexual allure, that seduces them both and finally leads them to their destruction" (Grant 276). Cummins appeared in two other popular films that happen to be personal favorites of mine, the widely celebrated horror cult film *Night of the Demon* (1957) with Dana Andrews and directed by Jacques Tourneur, and *Hell Drivers* (1957) with Stanley Baker and Patrick McGoohan (famous for *Danger Man* and *The Prisoner*).

I really like the premise of the story, "*Gun Crazy* is a case history of a man whose gun fixation dates from his childhood. He is not a bad kid, flashbacks informs us, since he does not use guns to kill living things" (Hirsch 195). That alone was enough to make an interesting story to explore, but the film ultimately follows down a dark path of ruin and eventual death that is more then orchestrated by Bart's deranged wife. Ironically, the two trick shooters could have had a thriving life together by using their talents with a gun for good purposes, but instead of going straight, they ended up being famous anyway as harden criminals on the run from the pursuing law. Their ultimate fate leads them through a dark and foreboding swamp, sheer desperation across their faces as they try to escape the police chasing them, an eerie fog closes in around them, as they realize they have no where else left to run to. A great ending to their life of crime and a sad reminder that crime does not pay in the end.

I greatly enjoyed the different (indie-style) techniques used in the film like flashbacks, showing Bart's past, motives, and fears. We get to understand why he feels the way he does about guns. Another appealing factor in *Gun Crazy* is the clever use of POV shots between Laurie and Bart during their gun competition scene, the picturesque montage of Bart and his wife's honeymoon, showing the passage of time, and spending all of their money. Even when Bart and Laurie are eating out at the diner, we are presented with a POV shot of the grill cook's representation as we see Bart and Laurie at the far end of the diner waiting for their burgers.

The film *Gun Crazy* is loaded with what we would call today as classic "guerrilla filmmaking" involving low budgets, small crews, minimal props, and shooting scenes quickly at real locations (outdoors) in public (example: Bart and Laurie rob a bank in real-time with the camera all the while is in the backseat during the whole scene arriving into town and leaving), and without much warning, but simply getting the shot, and moving on to the next scene. This kind of filmmaking is encouraging to film students who want to shoot on a shoestring budget using clever styles to get the job done. Gun Crazy in 1998 was selected for preservation in the United States National Film Registry by the Library of Congress as being culturally, historically, or aesthetically significant. *Gun Crazy* is truly a gem in the B-movie category of film noir and noteworthy for its stylistic approach.

9

D.O.A.

The introduction of the main character in *D.O.A.* is cleverly done by purposely showing only the backside of Frank Bigelow as he walks through the lengthy, maze-like police station, Bigelow eventually locates the homicide department, he enters, his face still hidden from camera view, and not made visible until he sits down, as author John Grant observes in his book *A Comprehensive Encyclopedia of Film Noir: The Essential Reference Guide*, "to report a murder - "Mine." The rest of the movie tells in flashback..." (Grant 191). A great opening and great line of a compelling mystery that gives the audience a taste of things to come and sets the tone for the entire film thereafter.

The real story of *D.O.A.* is told in flashbacks, Frank Bigelow (Edmond O'Brien) is from the small town of Banning, near Palm Springs, he runs an accountant/income tax business there, and decides to leave on vacation without his fiancée Paula Gibson (Pamela Britton), who is also his secretary. He goes to San Francisco, the big city, to where all the fun and action allegedly is waiting for the taking. Bigelow is there for freedom's sake, to live a few days on the wild side, and enjoy all the whims of a free agent. He visits a downtown bar with new acquaintances, has a few drinks, and by next morning discovers he has been fatally poisoned by someone. Several doctors inform him that a *luminous toxin* is slowly killing him, with no cure and perhaps only 48 hours to live, with that devastating news, Bigelow flees on a quest to discover who murdered him and why.

Bigelow relentlessly, pursues all the clues across cities (San Francisco to Los Angeles) to piece together the reasons why somebody would want to kill in the first place. Step by step, meeting everyone who is connected to the sudden death of Mrs. Philips' (Lynn Baggett) husband, and the shipment of iridium. Frantically, Bigelow pushes hard for answers, even at the risk of his own life while encountering criminals and murderers to get to the truth before he really dies. He does eventually get to the awful truth, part of a cover-up to conceal the shipment of iridium, Mrs. Philips' secret love affair, and the death of her husband. But before time runs out, Bigelow, now fully armed with a gun, manages to track down his own murderer, and in a climatic gunfight in the famous and moody Bradbury Building, shoots him dead, before he goes to the police station, to confess his murderer's crime and his own.

The film *D.O.A.* is a classic film noir mystery with a compelling storyline and a twist on the familiar theme of the manhunt scenario, only in this case not by a hard-boiled P.I. getting paid to solve a crime, but instead the investigator is the victim, and strictly motivated for personal reasons, not money. Like the cynical detective of earlier film noirs of the 1940s, the central character is determined to finding the whole truth, but the thriller *D.O.A.* embarks on yet a new path, where the main character is spurred on a mission to stop corruption and seeking vengeance, is only partly why such urgency is portrayed in the film, as Foster Hirsch points out in his book, *The Dark Side of the Screen: Film Noir*, "In *D.O.A.*, the investigator is dying of poison, and so his search to find his killer is quite literally a race against time" (Hirsch 174).

For the character Bigelow in *D.O.A.*, it is now a frantic hunt through the wild city, nothing else matters to him anymore, his only quest is in finding who is responsible for his soon-to-be death. So the tone and disposition of Bigelow, once a small town accountant, observed by Hirsch, has drastically changed, "The investigating hero can be portrayed in a variety of emotional tones, from the utter coolness and poise of Bogart's Spade and Marlowe to highly-strung questers, such as Edmond O'Brien in *D.O.A.* (who wants to find out who poisoned him and why) or Glenn Ford in *The Big Heat* (tracking the gang that killed his wife), who have a strong personal investment in cracking the case" (Hirsch 168). This also gives Bigelow a chance to reflect on his otherwise routine, unfaithful, and drab life. His journey to finding his murderer actually gives meaning to the last moments of his life and his renewed appreciation and love for his girlfriend, Paula Gibson.

Ussing real locations gave the film *D.O.A.* a sense of realism and foreboding, as Hirsch explains, "....many films in the late forties and early fifties (*Panic in the Street, Side Street, The Naked City, D.O.A., The Window, Night and the City*), Expressionist motifs invaded location shooting, transforming the real city into moody echoes of the claustrophobic studio-created urban landscape" (Hirsch 67). Placing the story in pristine San Francisco, by day it's busy, exciting, and peaceful, but by nightfall it's alive with the unknown mixed with flashing neon lights that promises even more action. Lavish parties, drunken businessmen and women, bars and nightclubs, and cold hearted killers all mingle together under the jive music at The Fisherman. This is the harsh reality small-towner like Bigelow faces when he wonders into the unforgiving depths of the concrete city.

The film *D.O.A* is directed by Rudolph Maté (1898–1964), a well "respected cinematographers in the industry, Polish-born Rudolph Maté entered the film business after his graduation from the University of Budapest (in philosophy). He worked in Hungary as an assistant cameraman for Alexander Korda and later worked throughout Europe with noted cameraman Karl Freund" (imdb, bio). Maté's impressive work quickly raised him to cinematographer status in 1928, and he "was soon working on some of Europe's most prestigious films, cementing his reputation as one of the continent's premier cinematographers" (imdb, bio). He arrived in America in the 1930s and landed contracts with Fox and Samuel Goldwyn. Maté made his directorial debut with the film *It Had to Be You* (1947) and the notable effort, *The Dark Past* (1948), he switched to directing films full-time thereafter, "unfortunately, while many of his directorial efforts were visually impressive (especially his sci-fi epic *When Worlds Collide* (1951)), the films themselves were for the most part undistinguished, with his best work probably being the film-noir classic *D.O.A.* (1950)" (imdb, bio).

As both director and cinematographer, Rudolph Maté had a long and distinguish career across two continents, he was a master of obtaining a visual style and tone appropriate for each film as director of photography and directing over 30 films in his lifetime. Though Maté was not a very strong director or consistent with his overall personal style of directing, nevertheless, he was nominated five times for the Oscars. The film *D.O.A.* directed by Maté is considered the best version, film noir critic Grant would agree, list two other versions made after, "remakes include *Color Me Dead* (1969), director Eddie Davis, with Tom Tryon, Carolyn Jones, Rick Jason, and Tony Ward, and *D.O.A.* (1988)" (Grant 191). The 1988 version starred Dennis Quaid, Meg Ryan, Charlotte Rampling, and Daniel Stern, and was directed by Annabel Jankel and Rocky Morton.

D.O.A. starts off typical and ordinary at first, but quickly descends into a nightmare situation as a doomed man must locate who poisoned him and why, as Grant mentions, "The movie's premise is enchanting and its execution expert" (Grant 191). The desperately paced plot of *D.O.A* was written by American screenwriters Clarence Greene and Russell Rouse. Often collaborating together on stories, screenplays, and off-beat films, the two were more than just writers, Greene was also a producer, and Rouse was also a director and producer of original work for both film and television. They first collaborated on the film *The Town Went Wild* (1944), and as screenwriters on *D.O.A.* (1950). They soon teamed up again on several film noirs, taking on the roles of screenwriter, producer, and director, most notably on *The Well* (1951) for which they were nominated for the Academy Award, and later made *The Thief* (1952), *Wicked Woman* (1953), *New York Confidential* (1955), and *House of Numbers* (1957).

Both men were highly talented and ambitious, "in the late 1950s, Greene and Rouse formed a production company, Greene-Rouse Productions, which created the film noir television series

Tightrope that ran for one season (1959 - 1960) as well as two films in the 1960s" (Wikipedia). Greene and Rouse made other impressive work, they produced two westerns, (*The Fastest Gun Alive* (1956), one of my favorite films starring Glenn Ford, Jeanne Crain and Broderick Crawford, and *Thunder in the Sun* (1959), *Pillow Talk* (1959), based on their screenplay, starring Rock Hudson, Doris Day, and Tony Randall. The classic film noir *D.O.A* has been regarded as Greene and Rouse's best and most talked about film collaboration of their careers. "That film has also been remade several times, and they were credited as writers on two of them: the Australian remake *Color Me Dead* from 1969 and the *D.O.A* remake of 1988" (Wikipedia).

Ernest Laszlo (1898 - 1984) was the cinematographer for *D.O.A*, originally born in Budapest, Austria-Hungary; he became a cinematographer in the late1920s and continued until 1977. "Best-known for his striking black-and-white cinematography for directors Robert Aldrich and Stanley Kramer, cinematographer Ernest Laszlo was a painstaking technician and a true artist who eschewed Hollywood glamour to bring a refreshing naturalism to his films " (TCM). Laszlo made over 60 films, he was a master in black and white film and equally adept in color, and some of his most exceptional works were, *Hold Back the Dawn* (1941), *The Major and the Minor* (1942), *D.O.A.* (1950) and *Stalag 17* (1953).

"Laszlo began working for Aldrich in 1954 with two Technicolor Burt Lancaster Westerns, *Apache* and *Vera Cruz*. The gritty black-and-white style associated with the two collaborators was established with *Kiss Me Deadly* (1955), Aldrich's film-noir treatment of the Mickey Spillane crime thriller. Other memorable Aldrich/Laszlo collaborations in this vein included The *Big Knife* (1955) and *Ten Seconds to Hell* (1959)" (TCM). Laszlo was nominated eight times for an Oscar and won for Best Cinematography for *Ship of Fools* (1966). "Four of Laszlo's nominations were for color films, proving that he worked just as effectively with a full palette. The science-fiction adventures

Film Noir: The Best of The Classics

Fantastic Voyage (1966) and *Logan's Run* (1976) gave full rein to his colorful imagination" (TCM).

Incidentally, I have been a fan of Laszlo's cinematography for years and never really knew it until this review, a few of his films I really like are, *Road to Rio* (1947), with Bing Crosby, Bob Hope, and Dorothy Lamour, *D.O.A.* (1950), *Houdini* (1953), starring Tony Curtis and Janet Leigh, *Stalag 17* (1953), *Vera Cruz* (1954), *The Naked Jungle* (1954), *Kiss Me Deadly* (1955), *Attack of the Puppet People* (1958), *It's a Mad, Mad, Mad, Mad World* (1963), *Ship of Fools* (1965), *Fantastic Voyage* (1966), *Airport* (1970), and my favorite most of all, *Logan's Run* (1976).

Edmond O'Brien (1915- 1985) plays the doomed Frank Bigelow in *D.O.A.*, a prolific actor from a bygone era of filmmaking. O'Brien was famous on Broadway and radio, in film and television, and of veteran in the U.S. Army Air Force during World War II. Born in Brooklyn, New York, he started taking drama in high school and while attending Columbia University, he majored in dramatic arts, earned a scholarship to attend the Neighborhood Playhouse School of the Theatre, and by age 21 was already appearing on Broadway with a deep commanding voice which gave him more depth and range.

By the late 1930s, began O'Brien's film career as a supporting actor, *The Hunchback of Notre Dame* (1939), unfortunately O'Brien wasn't leading man material, but between his excellent work in radio and supporting roles in film, have gained him considerable respect as a character actor. Some of his best films are *The Killers* (1946), *White Heat* (1949), *D.O.A.* (1950), *The Barefoot Contessa* (1954), a role O'Brien won an Academy Award for Best Supporting Actor, and another excellent film two years later based the novel by George Orwell, *1984* (1956), the first cinema rendition of the story, directed by Michael Anderson, with Donald Pleasence, Jan Sterling, and Michael Redgrave, and other great films by O'Brien include, *The Man Who Shot Liberty Valance* (1962), *Birdman of Alcatraz* (1962), *The Longest Day* (1962), *Seven Days in May* (1964), nominated for his role as an alcoholic U.S. senator, *Fantastic Voyage* (1966), and *The Wild Bunch* (1969).

Pamela Britton (1923 - 1974) plays Paula Gibson, Frank Bigelow's secretary and love interest in *D.O.A.*, a Broadway actress, Britton's most popular films were, *Anchors Aweigh* (1945) with Frank Sinatra, Kathryn Grayson, and Gene Kelly, *D.O.A.* (1950), and *Watch the Birdie* (1950). Britton later switched over to doing television, and appeared in numerous TV shows like, *Blondie* (1957), *77 Sunset Strip* (1960), *Peter Gunn* (1961), and my personal favorite as Mrs. Lorelei Brown on *My Favorite Martian* (1963-1966) with Bill Bixby and Ray Walston. Britton would later rejoin Bill Bixby on an episode of his TV series, *The Magician* (1973–1974).

Luther Adler played the mysterious Majak, a suave and cool character who does not like people investigating his personal business like the way Frank Bigelow does in the film *D.O.A.*, he is impressed by Bigelow's fearlessness and dogged determination, but he still tries to kill him anyway. Adler is perfect for this role and has had a long film and television career since 1937. His most prominent roles in cinema were *House of Strangers* (1949), *D.O.A.* (1950), *The Desert Fox: The Story of Rommel* (1951), and *Absence of Malice* (1981).

In my final thoughts, *D.O.A.* rest solely on the excellent performance by Edmond O'Brien, an underrated actor, portrays a dying man's plight to solve a murder, his own. The clever look of the overall film directed by Rudolph Maté and his accomplice, cinematographer Ernest Laszlo is spot on. The film *D.O.A.* is filled with impressive off-beat sequences, the intriguing, opening shot of Frank Bigelow comes to mind, instantly our curiosity is peaked, and his opening line is unforgettable. The atmospheric jive club "The Fisherman" splashing nautical theme with black musicians providing jazzy music to mostly a white hipster crowd. The shocking and revealing dialogue between Bigelow and Dr. MacDonald (Frank Gerstle), Dr. MacDonald states, "This is a case for homicide." Bigelow asked, "Homicide?" "I don't think you fully understand, Bigelow. You've been murdered."

The action scenes in public of Bigelow running for his very life, the tense shootout in the warehouse district, and the fact that everyone he meets is lying to him, but Bigelow is as persistent and dogmatic as TV's Detective Columbo (Peter Falk), and shrewdly solves his own murder case. Bigelow meets the crazy gunman, Chester (Neville Brand), is not your average thug, he really is a psycho. The grieving Mrs. Philips (Lynn Baggett), is actually a "black widow" having an affair and knows who killed her husband, and using the interior of the ever popular Bradbury Building with its 19th century architecture in downtown Los Angeles, used in so many famous films (*Blade Runner*) and television (*The Outer Limits* episode "Demon with a Glass Hand"), with its light-filled Victorian count rising 50 feet with open-cage elevators, marble stairs and ornate iron railings, evoke the film noir themes.

To summarize, what makes this a great film noir mystery is its unpredictability. The film keeps the suspense going all the way to end of the movie. As we watch Bigelow come to grips with his looming death within 48 hours, he races against time to find answers on who poisoned him and why, meeting a host of shady characters, partygoers, lairs, and thugs that inhabit an underworld of music, corruption, and deceit, which only compliments the suspenseful nature of the story, and by not letting go of the fact that this nightmare is happening to an average man who's simple life is suddenly turned upside-down, and doomed to died by a someone else's greed. The film *D.O.A.* makes for an excellent edge on your seat mystery/thriller and is worth having in your film noir collection with an unforgettable premise. And a warning to never leave your beer unattended.

T.S.Garp

10

IN A LONELY PLACE

The film *In a Lonely Place* has great performances, witty dialog, superb cast, great chemistry between Humphrey Bogart and Gloria Grahame and some clever touches by director Nicholas Ray. The murder mystery film noir classic, *In a Lonely Place* (1950) is a depiction of the nature of a psychopath and a character that defies understanding. As film noir themes go, there are many states of evil in literature (pulp fiction), film, and in real life. The motive for murder is usually centered on jealousy, greed, conflict, revenge, and hatred. Even a common criminal is only interested in steeling or gaining wealth, killing for them, is an afterthought, if caught or trapped.

However, there is another sort of evil that comes from those unpredictable and deranged minds that actively seek out victims for no apparent reason, but may be triggered by the killer's own confused thoughts, sudden rage, and anti-social behavior. These characters are impulsive, dangerous, and living on the edge of society, and in most cases existing right amongst us in everyday life, unsuspecting, acting normal at first and largely unnoticed until their murderous fury comes out, and by that time, it's too late.

But a typical psychopath is seemingly charming, very normal looking, and they tend to make a good first impression on others. Nonetheless, they are egotistical, deceitful and untrustworthy, and their apparent average demeanor hides insanity that no one can see clearly. Evil like this is irreversible, beyond understanding, and beyond explanation, as mental illness slowly sets in consuming the rational mind into a murderous, violent mind. This is exactly what Dixon Steele (Humphrey Bogart) is accused of in the film and the aftereffects will leave him in a lonely place he can never come back from, as observed in *The Dark Side of the Screen: Film Noir* by Foster Hirsch, "The lonely place in *In a Lonely Place* is the isolation enforced on the Hollywood screenwriter (Humphrey Bogart) by his anti-social behavior. His irrational explosions make him the likely suspect in a murder case and also alienate a neighbor (Gloria Grahame) who has grown romantically attached to him" (Hirsch 195).

This is one of the better unknown roles that Bogart has played on screen (a prelude to his Oscar nominating role in *The Caine Mutiny* in 1954), as a neurotic, ill-tempered, and very paranoid screenwriter who has a problem with snapping at people and getting into fist fights as quickly as saying hello to someone. Even with his devoted love interest, the alluring and calming nature of Laurel Gray (Gloria Grahame) can't hold back his rage and downfall, as John Grant mentions in his book *A Comprehensive Encyclopedia of Film Noir: The Essential Reference Guide,* "This powerful movie lacks any happy ending - both principals are destined for lonely places - and offers one of Grahame's most sensitive performances" (Grant 316).

Dixon Steele (Humphrey Bogart) is a screenwriter looking for a comeback, but instead is plagued by his own self-destructive and uncontrollable temper, that later makes him the prime suspect in a murder case. Given the opportunity to do another screenplay based on a book, Steele ask Mildred Atkinson (Martha Stewart) to come to his place to orally recite the book (he hates to read something he isn't interested in), and she does (she breaks off her dinner date with Henry Kessler (Jack Reynolds). The next day, the police question Steele, and judging by his lack of sympathy and concern for the young victim, they immediately think the cynical Hollywood screenwriter had something to do with it, but a neighbor living next door, Laurel Gray (Gloria Grahame), informed them that she has seen the young lady leave Steele's apartment just after midnight. The police investigation continues and theirs eyes are still set on somehow nailing Dixon Steele for murder.

Gradually, a romance between Steele and Gray blossoms. An old war buddy, who just happens to be one of the homicide officers investigating the murder of Mildred Atkinson, Det. Sgt. Brub Nicolai (Frank Lovejo) invites him over for dinner with his wife,

Sylvia. Later, after dinner, Steele is asked how he thinks the murder was committed, and he complies by verbally reenacting the death scene in a convincing and compelling, if not hypnotic voice, the display is so vivid, as he suggests using the Nicolai's as props that nearly chokes the life out of Sylvia. The police remind Gray that Steele has a violent history and to be careful with him. But she is devoted to Steele, her "Dix" and believes him to be completely innocent.

Steele is head over heels for Gray and is instantly inspired to write another screenplay. Even though with Gray's companionship and constant love, Steele is unable to hide his hidden fury and violent nature from her forever. Soon his paranoia increases as the police still seem interested in him and in a fit of uncontrollable anger speeds away down the highway, nearly getting in a car accident, and almost beating a another man to death. Laurel Gray suddenly becomes worried about Steele's unpredictable behavior, seeing the rage in him, and plans to run away before they get married. But Steele proposes marriage, fearful of starting a fight, she reluctantly agrees, and during a celebration party for the engaged couple, Steele slaps his agent for taking his finished script without telling him first, totally disrupting the supposedly happy moment.

In fear of her life, Gray returns to her home without Steele, and packs her suitcase to leave town. Dixon Steele arrives, and confronts her and wonders why she is leaving him, and in furious fight, his temper almost kills her. Just then the telephone rings, and a disenchanted Steele answers it, Det. Nicolai calls to inform them Henry Kessler, Mildred Atkinson's boyfriend, confessed to the murder. Steele gives the phone to Laurel Gray, he silently leaves her apartment, and she learns the truth about the murder, but it's too late, the damage has been done. There will be neither wedding, nor any happiness between them anymore. Her Dix has left for good, never to return again.

In A Lonely Place is directed by Nicholas Ray (1911 - 1979), he was an American film director best known for the film *Rebel*

Film Noir: The Best of The Classics

Without a Cause (1955) starring James Dean and Natalie Wood, and praised for his work on *They Live by Night* (1948), *In a Lonely Place* (1950), *Johnny Guitar* (1954), *Bigger Than Life* (1956), *Bitter Victory* (1957), *King of Kings* (1961), *55 Days at Peking* (1963), and the experimental masterpiece, *We Can't Go Home Again* (1973). Ray made several contributions to film noir like *In a Lonely Place*, and most notably with films *A Woman's Secret* (1949), *On Dangerous Ground* (1951), and *Born to Be Bad* (1950).

But by the 1960s, Ray had health problems associated with drinking and drug abuse, he retired from filmmaking, and got a teaching position at Harpur College of Arts and Sciences at Binghamton University in 1971. Together with his filmmaking students they produced the autobiographical film *We Can't Go Home Again,* rough cuts were released, but Ray continued to edit the film until his death in 1979. Ray's skill of filmmaking can still be felt on new generations of filmmakers, "Ray's compositions within the CinemaScope frame and use of color are particularly well-regarded. Ray was an important influence on the French New Wave, with Jean-Luc Godard famously writing in a review of *Bitter Victory*, "cinema is Nicholas Ray" (Wikipedia). Even though the *In a Lonely Place* was moderately unsuccessful on release and the cinematography by Burnett Guffey was first-rate, the film has gained momentum over the years, and is today regarded by many as among film noir's finest.

The film is based on American crime writer, Dorothy B. Hughes' novel of the same name. Hughes has been often called the queen of noir for her excellent crime novels and crafting psychological suspense into every story. "Hughes wrote fourteen crime and detective novels, primarily in the hardboiled and noir styles, and is best known for the novels *In a Lonely Place* (1947) and *Ride the Pink Horse* (1946). Three of her novels were made into movies: *The Fallen Sparrow* in 1943 starring John Garfield, *In a Lonely Place* in 1950 directed by Nicholas Ray and starring Humphrey Bogart, and *Ride the Pink Horse* in 1947 directed by and starring Robert Montgomery, which was also remade in 1964 for TV as *The Hanged Man*" (Wikipedia).

Screenwriters Edmund H. North and Andrew Solt wrote the adaptation for the Dorothy B. Hughes novel. North's writing career spans more than 40 years, he wrote the screenplay for the science-fiction classic *The Day the Earth Stood Still* (1951) and came up with the line: Klaatu barada nikto. He also shared an Academy Award for Best Original Screenplay with Francis Ford Coppola for *Patton* (1970). Andrew Solt is best remembered for his screenplays for *The Jolson Story* (1946), *Joan of Arc* (1948), *Little Women* (1949), and *In a Lonely Place* (1950).

Legendary actor Humphrey Bogart (1899- 1957) plays the troubled screenwriter, Dixon Steele, accused of murder and inflicted with sudden bouts of rages in the classic film noir, *In A Lonely Place*. Bogart was born in New York, began acting on Broadway in the 1920s, started doing minor film roles in the 1930s, and by 1936, got his major breakout role in *The Petrified Forest*. Bogart personified his portrayal of hard core criminals and lethal gangsters in Hollywood movies thereafter, solidifying his early career as a heavy lead in such films like *The Great O'Malley* (1937), *Dead End* (1937), *Crime School* (1938) and *King of the Underworld* (1939). For many years, Bogart was typecast in these B-movies, but by the 1940s, his career will take a turn for the better, starting with an interesting co-starring role in the film noir, *They Drive By Night* (1940). The very next year, Bogart took the lead role in the popular film, *High Sierra* (1941) a part George Raft turned down. Bogart quickly rose to leading man status after his excellent performances in *The Maltese Falcon* (1941) and *Casablanca* (1942).

More outstanding and landmark roles followed for Bogart, such as in *Sahara* (1943), *To Have and Have Not* (1944) with Lauren Bacall, *The Big Sleep* (1946), *Dead Reckoning* (1947), *Dark Passage* (1947), *The Treasure of the Sierra Madre* (1948), *Key Largo* (1948), *In a Lonely Place* (1950), *The African Queen* (1951), *The Caine Mutiny* (1954), *Sabrina* (1954), *We're No*

Film Noir: The Best of The Classics

Angels (1955), *The Desperate Hours* (1955), and his last film, *The Harder They Fall* (1956). Bogart won the Academy Award for *The African Queen*, was nominated for his role in *Casablanca* and *The Caine Mutiny*. Bogart married Lauren Bacall in 1945 until his death from cancer in 1957.

Bogart during his entire film career has played a variety of diverse roles, some of which were characters out of control, like the "role of a victim in *Dark Passage*, of a criminal in *Conflict*, and of a crackpot in *In A Lonely Place*, Bogart coves the noir spectrum" (Hirsch 151). Bogart is most famous for playing smart, witty, cynical, private investigators that are always cool under pressure, and have an air of confidence about them. However so, Bogart's portrayal of the angry character in the film that is so removed from society and out of touch with reality is so compelling to watch as Steele is disliked by the police, fights with strangers and friends, and ultimately, thoroughly alienates his girlfriend who later breaks off their engagement. "Although lesser known than his other work, Bogart's performance is considered by many critics to be among his finest and the film's reputation has grown over time along with Ray's" (Wikipedia).

The role of Laurel Gray is played by actress Gloria Grahame (1923 - 1981) as the love interest of the hot-tempered screenwriter, Steele. Grahame is a perfect femme fatale to star opposite Bogart in a film noir such as this, she's attractive, mysterious, and has a combination of good-girl to bad-girl qualities, only this time she is the alluring neighbor next door that eventually becomes the most important woman in Steele's life. Grahame had an extraordinary career in Hollywood as, "a femme fatale with extraordinary carnal allure, Gloria Grahame electrified moviegoers with her turns as venal, sexually aggressive women in such films as *Crossfire* (1947), *In a Lonely Place* (1950) and *The Bad and the Beautiful* (1952), which earned her a Best Supporting Actress Oscar" (TCM).

Some of Grahame's best and noteworthy films are *It's a Wonderful Life* (1946), *Crossfire* (1947), *In a Lonely Place* (1950), *The Greatest Show on Earth* (1952), *The Bad and the Beautiful* (1952), *The Glass Wall* (1953), *The Big Heat* (1953), *Human Desire* (1954), *Oklahoma!* (1965), and *The Man Who Never Was* (1956). Grahame throughout her acting profession, has played "sexually confident if emotionally unstable women, and essentially repeated that role throughout the 1940s and 1950s, which marked her heyday in Hollywood. Few actresses could present such an openly wanton image as Grahame, whose heavy-lidded eyes and permanently curled lip - the result of botched surgery - lent her a physical gravitas other actresses lacked" (TCM). She could easily switch from vile temptress to innocent damsel in distress quite effectively.

By the 1960s and 1970s, Grahame switched to mainly doing TV roles and the occasional movie, but for me seeing her in an episode of the original *Outer Limits* television series, *The Guests* (1964), where she played a forgotten film star living in the past, which some say Grahame was spoofing her own fading career in the 1960s, was a delight as the classic Outer Limits series expressed a sc-fi film noir quality. Even so, Grahame is best remembered for her film noir and femme fatale roles that capitalized her trademarks of alluring, brooding, loyal, available, ravenous femininity.

In my research for this review, I discovered that the book differs from the actual film. The novel by Dorothy B. Hughes is a psychological crime story where we're introduced to the killer from the get-go and given a point of view of the serial killer (Steele) as the author describes his motives and feelings before he murders someone. I found that quite interesting, and the fact that the screenplay made Dixon Steele seem the most likely suspect because of his anti-social behavior and constant rage, but instead the film adoption presents us with another suspect (Henry Kessler) under the radar, who is the actual killer in the film and not Steele at all. A great misdirection or twist, but a sad final outcome for the character Steele, who loses the woman he has been dreaming about all his life. I think the performances from both leading actors were great, Humphrey Bogart and Gloria Grahame, had wonderful chemistry, Bogart was believable as the over-rattled writer with an unseemly temper, and Grahame as the concern, yet devoted love interest, who later feared for her life. A great film noir with a compelling story where the killer is not who you think it is. This film was selected for preservation in the United States National Film Registry by the Library of Congress as being "culturally, historically, or aesthetically significant" in 2007 and is now considered a classic film noir worth seeing.

11

KISS ME DEADLY

    The film opens up dramatically at night, with a mysterious barefoot woman running frantically down the vacant highway, wearing only a trench coat, as she tries to flag down anybody driving by. But no one is stopping to help her, so she stands in the middle of the road forming a symbolic X, forcing the next random car to react to her presence. A speeding Jaguar XK 120 Roadster driven by Mike Hammer (Ralph Meeker) nearly slams into her, he hit's the breaks, and steers the car into the dirt. "You almost wrecked my car!" he shouts angrily. The woman is out of breath, panic-stricken, and barely able to speak. He offers her a ride to the nearest bus stop, she gets in the convertible, and Hammer zooms down the dark highway (with backseat POV shot looking through the front windshield), as the film's credits creep down uncharacteristically from the top of the screen, combined with the sound of the engine, wind, the woman's heavy breathing, and Nat King Cole's *Rather Have the Blues* blaring from the Jaguar's radio. Hammer quickly learns she is wanted for escaping from a mental institution and has a terrible secret to tell.

    This is our introduction to private investigator Mike Hammer and the hysterical young woman, Christina Bailey (Cloris Leachman), he picks up on the road in Robert Aldrich's film noir thriller *Kiss Me Deadly* (1955) that is laced with violence no holds barred detective in a mystery satire, with political overtones of a real terror in the 1950s. The film really takes off as Christina mentions poetry, the secret, and warns Hammer that they might take her before reaching the bus stop, and to "remember her" if they do. Hammer is confused by her dire prediction and suddenly the highway is blocked by a dark car, causing the Jaguar to crash on the side of the road. Hammer is only semi-conscious when he hears Christina screaming in pain, as the strange men, who never show their faces to the camera, torture and kill her.

Film Noir: The Best of The Classics

Once Hammer recovers from his injuries, the police and government agents want to know what he knows about the girl, who died in the apparent car crash he was in. Hammer knows the young woman was murdered and he starts investigating as to why. This leads him to hunt down every clue and person associated with Christina Bailey, but Hammer is also being stalked by mysterious men and thugs like knife wielding attacker (Paul Richards). He locates Christina's apartment, finds more clues, and takes her poetry book (Sonnets of Christina Georgina Rossetti).

Hammer meets Christina's odd, but attractive roommate, Lily Carver aka Gabrielle (Gaby Rodgers), and claims to know nothing except her girlfriend was extremely scared about something horrible. His curiosity is peaked by the people that was connected with Christina and the mystery object, who all suddenly died in strange so-called accidents, leads him to gangster type Carl Evello (Paul Stewart), his sister Friday (Marian Carr), and hoodlums Sugar Smallhouse (Jack Lambert) and Charlie Max (Jack Elam). He is warned again to stop investigating, but Hammer persists in his own brutish way, especially when a friend he involves dies in another accident. But Hammer will not give up the quest for the "Great Whatzit" and pursues seeking answers. Somehow, Christina had managed to send Hammer a letter from the grave, a clue that she mailed to his office earlier, but Hammer is taken hostage, and brought to a remote Malibu house for interrogation.

In Malibu, Hammer is tied down in an X shape, and given truth serum. Hammer still has no idea if they are stealing gold, diamonds or drugs. They plan to kill him, but he swiftly escapes, back at his home he realizes there is a clue left in the written sonnet of Christina Georgina Rossetti. This leads him to the morgue where he obtains a key that was hidden inside Christina Bailey's body. The key takes him to the Hollywood Athletic Club, where it opens a storage locker that contains a mysterious black box. He feels it's hot to the touch; he barely opened a crack, and got severely burned by the white intense light instantly. He leaves the dangerous box where it is, Lily Carver disappears, and he earns later that she is an imposter (the real Lily Carver was murdered), and he gives the key to the authorities after hearing the words "Manhattan Project, Los Alamos, Trinity" realizing that he is dealing with deadly nuclear energy.

The murderous thieves have taken Hammer's girlfriend, Velda (Maxine Cooper), and he pursues more leads to Dr. Soberin's (Albert Dekker) Malibu cottage. In this climatic scene, Hammer confronts Gabrielle, who has a gun aimed at him; she has already killed the mysterious Dr. Soberin out of greed for the box. He knows that Dr. Soberin was the one who formulated the illegal theft of atomic material. But before he can pass that information to Gabrielle, she wickedly smiles at him, wants Hammer to come close to kiss her, but instead, shoots him point-blank, and he falls to the floor. She eagerly opens Pandora's Box to get at the wealth she thinks in hidden inside. A burning, blinding light fills the entire room, as Gabrielle's body is enveloped in a lethal dose of radiation, and she's set ablaze, screaming horrifically. Hammer, only wounded, manages to free his girlfriend from a locked room, and flee the house in flames. They race to the protection of the ocean as the house behind them explodes.

The film *Kiss Me Deadly* symbolically covers the hype of the Red Scare and the threat of nuclear war with Russia that dominated American's psyche in the 1950s. The plot of the movie is unlike any other film noir mystery, in that the actual goal of the criminals is not merely money or wealth, but the desire for supreme power and greed in the form of deadly atomic energy. The sought after prize is at first a great enigma, often referred to as the quest for the great whatzit, until it is revealed to be stolen nuclear power encased in a lead box, hot to the touch and lethal if let out, like the mythic Gorgon, its blinding glare could cause instant death, and its voice is that of a hideous hissing ear-piercing scream of wind and light so powerful is this nightmare, that it could literally destroy the whole world.

Actor Ralph Meeker did an excellent portrayal in this film that is debatably the best version of author Mickey Spillane's antihero

Film Noir: The Best of The Classics

Mike Hammer. But one has to ask after watching the film, did director Robert Aldrich enjoy making this movie or did he brutally shape it into a film that is truly deadly? The main protagonist is unforgiving, self-centered, and unlike any other hard-boiled detective we've come to know in film noirs. Aldrich and screenwriter A. I. Bezzerides, take extreme liberties on rewriting the main character from the book. But the classic villains and femme fatales are all there, only this time they are more disturbing and crazier than ever. Still, despite the convoluted plot and stark look of the film, *Kiss Me Deadly* is by far one of the best film noirs to arrive in the 1950s that is both culturally relevant and up-to-date on the fear of the Atomic Age.

Film noir, during the hype of its era, seems to break new ground every few years with its independent style and often controversial filmmaking, and the film *Kiss Me Deadly* is no exception, as John Grant notes this in his book, *A Comprehensive Encyclopedia of Film Noir: The Essential Reference Guide*, "one odd feature of the movie is that the opening credits run backward" (Grant 354). In film noir the play on light and shadow is very important, characteristic framing, and the set design all convey the mood of the story, and the strange hidden signs are mentioned by Foster Hirsch in his book, *The Dark Side of the Screen: Film Noir*, "In addition to its symbolic use of ordinary environment, noir also riles on surreal and exotic settings" (Hirsch 86), This could be the way a character is standing or sitting, a striking piece of architecture, a strange forbidding road or an abandoned warehouse, not just simple background, but a key element in the film noir story, even an isolated house in Malibu can't be trusted where crime and murder is commented, and perhaps the end of the world as is implied in the "apocalyptic imagery at the end of *Kiss Me Deadly*, where Pandora's Box contains an atomic blast" (Hirsch 86). Some of action scenes and evil decadence portrayed in the film seems over-the-top. "The contrasting late noir tendency is exaggeration tinged with satire. Such films as *Kiss Me Deadly*,

The Big Combo, Screaming Mimi, Touch of Evil, all represent noir's decadence" (Hirsch 202).

Robert Aldrich directed *Kiss Me Deadly*, he started working on films in the early 1940s at RKO and soon rose to assistant director status. By the 1950s he started directing and scripting television, but made his directorial debut in film with the *Big Leaguer* (1953). Aldrich then directed two very popular Western films *Vera Cruz* (1954) and *Apache* (1954), both starring Burt Lancaster. He than shifted gears to make two film noirs; *Kiss Me Deadly* (1955) and *The Big Knife* (1956). But Aldrich is best known for two chilling psychological thrillers *What Ever Happened to Baby Jane* (1962) and *Hush, Hush Sweet Charlotte* (1965), both starring Bette Davis. Aldrich directed a variety of films covering any genre, some of his best are *The Flight of the Phoenix* (1965), *The Dirty Dozen* (1967), *The Killing of Sister George* (1968), *Emperor of the North Pole* (1973), *The Longest Yard* (1974), and *Twilight's Last Gleaming* (1977).

Aldrich's sense of narrative style is a conflict between characters living in a harsh environment, whereupon the main focus is on personal ideology, the explosive tension shared by the people in the story, all conveying their own dissatisfaction and position regarding life in the present world. Aldrich blurs the lines between who is really good and evil, for the hero or antihero in his films go beyond cynical and sinful, they are motivated by their own code of ethics and pursue strictly egotistical goals. This philosophy translated well for him, when he directed his first film noir, "having Aldrich at the helm, *Kiss Me Deadly* is not only better noir than many, despite its unpromising substrate, but also has been more widely discussed than most" (Grant 354). Aldrich's two most influential films are incidentally *Vera Cruz* and *Kiss Me Deadly*.

The screenwriter for *Kiss Me Deadly* is A. I. Bezzerides (1908 - 2007). A very gifted novelist and screenwriter, who was an electrical /communications engineer before he took up screenwriting full-time. He had written several novels in the 1930s and 1940s, and Hollywood later wanted to adapt one of them to film, starting with his book *The Long Haul* (1938), which later became *They Drive by Night* (1940), starring Humphrey Bogart, George Raft, and Ann Sheridan. Offered a high paying writing contract, thereafter, began his screenwriting career in Hollywood with such films as *Desert Fury* (1947), *Thieves' Highway* (1949), based on Bezzerides' third novel, *Thieves' Market* (1949), *On Dangerous Ground* (1952), *Beneath the 12 Mile Reef* (1953), *Track of the Cat* (1954), and *Kiss Me Deadly* (1955).

"Bezzerides' most famous script is *Kiss Me Deadly* (1955), a masterful and influential film noir. He transformed the novel by Mickey Spillane into an apocalyptic, atomic-age paranoia film noir. When asked about his script, and his decision to make "the great whatsit" the Pandora's Box objective of a ruthless cast of characters, Bezzerides commented: "People ask me about the hidden meanings in the script, about the A-bomb, about McCarthyism, what does the poetry mean, and so on. And I can only say that I didn't think about it when I wrote it . . . I was having fun with it. I wanted to make every scene, every character, interesting. A girl comes up to Ralph Meeker, I make her a nympho. She grabs him and kisses him the first time she sees him. She says, "You don't taste like anybody I know." I'm a big car nut, so I put in all that stuff with the cars and the mechanic. I was an engineer, and I gave the detective the first phone answering machine in that picture. I was having fun" (Wikipedia).

American pulp fiction novelist, Mickey Spillane's book *Kiss Me, Deadly* (1952) which features private investigator Mike Hammer and is the bases for the film of the same name. Spillane's most famous character (Hammer) was introduced in his novel *I, the Jury* (1947). Spillane's detective Mike Hammer series were all bestsellers and sold more than 225 million copies worldwide. Spillane joined the ranks of other popular crime novelist like Dashiell Hammett and Raymond Chandler. But he also helped define the hardboiled literary genre once again, by inventing his main character Mike Hammer, who is unlike any other detective in crime fiction. Spillane's self-centered and cynical detective was no where near as moral as Sam Spade or Philip Marlowe, in fact, the character of Mike Hammer was more brutish and unforgiving as the crime world he occupied in. But still, Spillane's compelling detective stories were good enough to overlook Hammer's lack of restraints or bending the law to stop crime.

The cinematographer for *Kiss Me Deadly* is Ernest Laszlo (1898 - 1984), a classic cinematographer from the 1920s era of filmmaking and expert in German expressionistic lighting and shadows, known for his outstanding 'black-and-white' cinematography, and frequently teamed up with directors Robert Aldrich and Stanley Kramer. Some of his most brilliant works are *Hold Back the Dawn* (1941), *The Major and the Minor* (1942), *D.O.A.* (1950) and *Stalag 17* (1953). "Laszlo began working for Aldrich in 1954 with two Technicolor Burt Lancaster Westerns, *Apache* and *Vera Cruz*. The gritty black-and-white style associated with the two collaborators was established with *Kiss Me Deadly* (1955), Aldrich's film-noir treatment of the Mickey Spillane crime thriller. Other memorable Aldrich/Laszlo collaborations in this vein included *The Big Knife* (1955) and *Ten Seconds to Hell* (1959)" (TCM).

Laszlo did cinematography for these great films also like *Road to Rio* (1947), *Houdini* (1953), *Vera Cruz* (1954), *The Naked Jungle* (1954), *Attack of the Puppet People* (1958), *It's a Mad, Mad, Mad, Mad World* (1963), *Ship of Fools* (1965), *Fantastic Voyage* (1966), *Airport* (1970), and *Logan's Run* (1976). Laszlo was nominated eight times for an Oscar and won for Best Cinematography for *Ship of Fools* (1966). "Four of Laszlo's nominations were for color films, proving that he worked just as effectively with a full palette. The science-fiction adventures *Fantastic Voyage* (1966) and *Logan's Run* (1976) gave full rein to his colorful imagination" (TCM).

Ralph Meeker plays Mike Hammer in *Kiss Me Deadly* and does a very fine job of it too. Meeker was a Broadway actor in the 1940s, learned method acting, and appeared in the plays *A Streetcar Named Desire* and *Picnic*. Made his first two European

Film Noir: The Best of The Classics

films in 1951, *Teresa* and *Four in a Jeep*. However, even though Meeker's performances in plays and films were often highly praised, his good looks and charisma, he could never reach the stardom that eluded him or enjoy A-list parts in feature films. He soon became a bit of a character actor, playing equally villainous roles to the good hero, but his entire career has gained cult status by starring *Kiss Me Deadly*. His portrayal of "Hammer, at least as depicted in this movie, represents a sea change from the Philip Marlowe model of rumpled white knight, or even the flawed, amoral, but self-aware Sam Spade of *The Maltese Falcon* (1941); Hammer is a near cipher, a *bedroom dick* interested as much in extorting money from his malfeasant clients as in earning his living from investigation" (Grant 354).

Many film historians agree his representation of Mickey Spillane's Mike Hammer is most compelling to watch and in Meeker's other acclaimed role in Stanley Kubrick's unsettling depiction of war's insanity, *Paths of Glory* (1957), as Meeker plays a condemned World War I French soldier. Some of Ralph Meeker's best films are *The Naked Spur* (1953), *Kiss Me Deadly* (1955), *Paths of Glory* (1957), *The Dirty Dozen* (1967), *The St. Valentine's Day Massacre* (1967), *The Anderson Tapes* (1971), and the telefilm *The Night Stalker* (1972) with Darren McGavin.

Cloris Leachman plays Christina Bailey, the women running down the highway with no shoes on that Mike Hammer picks up at the opening of the film; this also marks her film debut. Leachman as been in show business since 1947 and is mainly famous for her numerous TV roles spanning over 60 years, particularly on the Mary Tyler Moore (1970 - 1977). But she is also well known in such films a *The Last Picture Show* (1971) and *Young Frankenstein* (1974). Even today, at 89 years old, Cloris Leachman continues to act in TV and film, and voice acting on major animation films.

For my final thoughts regarding *Kiss Me Deadly*, this is a superb, stylistic, hard-edged film noir classic, with surprising themes of apocalyptic doom, bordering on science fiction, but still a great murder mystery. The film captures the mood and the paranoia of the 1950s expertly, the violence of the main character displays the disillusionment by citizens of this time. I really like Mike Hammer, he is rough and unsympathetic, but so are his adversaries. He is trying to be tough in a world that got a bit scarier with the atomic bomb looming over every country and thugs lurking around every corner. Director Robert Aldrich gave us an indie-style, low-budget, vicious, fast-paced, Cold War fright film, that follows cynical private investigator Mike Hammer on the quest for the great whatzit. It is the Christina Rossetti poem about death that finally leads Hammer to the great whatzit, the symbol for doomsday.

This film is a mini-masterpiece, with skewed camera angles, POV shots, the Americana locations, extreme close-ups, now regarded as a cult classic, and has inspired several films like *Repo Man* (1984) and *Pulp Fiction* (1994). The film goes beyond just your average murder mystery; it's a thriller that packs a violent punch to the ribs and political message. The Kefauver Commission pronounced the film, *Kiss Me Deadly,* to be damaging to younger viewers, and that hindered a successful turnout back in 1955, but over time it has risen from the ashes to be thoroughly enjoyed, and deservingly so. By 1997 a lost version of *Kiss Me Deadly* with the original ending for the film was finally restored. In 1999, *Kiss Me Deadly* was selected for preservation in the United States National Film Registry by the Library of Congress as being "culturally, historically, or aesthetically significant." Famous French director, Francois Truffaut even praised the film for its originality. This is a film worth seeing again and again.

Film Noir: The Best of The Classics

12

THE BIG HEAT

The opening of *The Big Heat* begins with a shocking death, by way of an image of a revolver on a desk and a hand reaching out for it, the gun is lifted out of view, and a loud shot is fired. The faceless man's body falls upon the desktop, he has taken his own life out of desperation, and left his police badge and a suicide note. His wife, Bertha Duncan (Jeanette Nolan), alerted by the gunshot, comes into the room with a cold, dispassionate stare at her husband's corpse. She instantly picks up the last letter he wrote addressed to the D.A.'s office. Without hesitation or before telephoning the police, she calls Mike Lagana (Alexander Scourby), the notorious gangster kingpin who controls most of the city with extortion, terrorism, and criminal activity. With just a few strokes of her fingers on the dial, Mrs Duncan has joined the ranks of Lagana's organized crime syndicate.

The local police arrive at the Duncan house, the investigating homicide policeman is Det. Sgt. Dave Bannion (Glenn Ford), he wonders why no suicide note was left, and questions Mrs Duncan about what happen. Unbeknownst to Bannion, Mrs Duncan has been practicing at lying her way a good charade for him, showing great distress about her husband's sudden death through false tears, and insinuates that her husband Tom suffered from painful spills, and that he was unhappy for being secretly ill. Good cop Bannion at first believes this is a simple case of suicide, until he gets a tip from Tom Duncan's mistress, Lucy Chapman (Dorothy Green), who claims Tom was not suicidal or ill, but that he was planning to divorce his wife. Bannion holds her with contempt, a barfly, but because Bannion is a dedicated police detective, and morally ethical at this point, he revisited Mrs Duncan to try to get more facts about Tom's affairs, and inadvertently tells her about Chapman's claims.

The next day, Lucy Chapman is brutally murdered, and Bannion is mildly puzzled by her sudden death after talking to her only once. His boss tells him to leave the Duncan widow alone and stop asking too many questions. Still seeking the truth, Bannion undaunted, hit's *The Retreat* bar and club, and pursues the death of the Lucy Chapman. Stonewalled by the bartender and lack of his superior's interest in the case, he returns home to his domesticated life with his wife and daughter. Bannion's home is a perfect example of the urban 1950s American family unit, Katie Bannion (Jocelyn Brando) keeps the house clean, dinner on the table, and even drinks beer with her devoted husband. This lifestyle is a stark contrast to the lowly, filth and scum, Bannion has to deal with on the streets while doing his job. But during the night, in his suburban oasis, Bannion's wife receives a harassing phone call from Lagana's hoodlums.

Bannion storms right over to the Lagana estate, pushes his way in, and confronts Lagana himself. He accuses Lagana's involvement with Lucy Chapman and that there's a connection with Tom Duncan's death. Lagana threatens him with trespassing and vowels that Bannion will lose his job over this disruption in his mansion. Bannion is chastised by his boss, Lt. Ted Wilks (Willis Bouchey), for going over the line with Lagana, and warns him to stop, as this command is coming from upstairs. Bannion begins to wonder how many policemen in the department are on Lagana's payroll, and which are the good cops versus bad the ones. He returns home to his blissful life with his loving wife, and as he is about to tuck his daughter into bed, a horrific explosion shakes the house. His beautiful wife is killed from a car bomb planted in his car meant for him. Bannion's life is now turned upside down and he vows vengeance on those responsible for the death of his wife.

Afterwards, Bannion sends his daughter away, and he sells the house. He quits the police force after the Police Commissioner Higgins (Howard Wendell) and Lt. Ted Wilks tell him to forget the matter as it will take months to discover who murdered his wife. Bannion insist it was Lagana's organized crime syndicate that killed her, but Police Commissioner Higgins doesn't want to implicate Lagana. Now, more than ever, Bannion knows he is surrounded by crooked cops all the way to the top. He goes on the hunt for more clues that leads him to *The Retreat,* where he is an eyewitness to the vicious burning of a female customer, Doris (Carolyn Jones), by Vince Stone (Lee Marvin), Lagana's right-hand man. Bannion kicks the thugs out of the bar and he is followed by Stone's ditzy girlfriend, Debby Marsh (Gloria Grahame), who was left behind in the confusion. She flirts with him, impressed and delighted that he intervened on the poor Doris' behalf, and shows genuine interest in Bannion. But Bannion is on a dark path of hate and wants nothing to do with anyone connected with Lagana.

Upon Debby's return at Stone's apartment she is cornered and beaten by Stone for talking to Bannion. Unsatisfied, with her denial, Stone throws a pot of boiling coffee onto her pretty face, severely scolding it. She is rushed to the hospital screaming and in agony. She will never look as attractive again. Lagana wants no more loose-ends and orders Stone to kill her at the hospital. But Debby escapes, rushes over to Bannion's hotel, and hides out there. Debby is afraid they will try to kill her, she informs him that she is scarred for her life, and between her sobs, tells Bannion everything she knows, including names of officials corrupted by Lagana's crime ring. Bannion at first appears indifferent by her plight, his defiance to let go of his personal vendetta against all those of immoral conduct is strong, but his humanity flickers a little by Debby's fear and real pain, and he mildly response to being somewhat nice to her.

Debby gave away the whereabouts of Larry Gordon (Adam Williams), the young punk that calls himself a hit man for hired that planted the car bomb for the mob that accidentally killed his wife instead of him. Bannion arrives at Gordon's apartment and introduces himself with a right-cross, knocking Gordon to the floor. He easily overpowers Gordon, and proceeds to strangle him to death, but decides to get some answers first. Gordon pleads for his life and tells Bannion all he knows. Specifically, that Tom

Duncan was working for Lagana, and now Duncan's wife, Mrs Duncan, is now on that take with Lagana's crime syndicate. Later, the mob kill Gordon for talking his head off to Bannion, meanwhile, Bannion confronts Mrs Duncan at her house for the whole truth. But she openly confesses that she does not care about anything or anybody anymore, just as long as she gets paid. It's all about money and comfort for her, nothing else matters, not justice, not her marriage, not her moral obligations to rid society of criminals. Bannion nearly strangles her to death for withholding vital evidence on Lagana's crime activities, for lying to him, and joining the dark side of wickedness that had enveloped the entire city under mob rule.

He stops as the police arrive to check on Mrs Duncan. Later, he returns to his hotel, and brings Debby some food. Their relationship has turned into a sort of odd friendship, both emotionally injured, and seeking justice. In a casual conversation, Bannion informs Debby if Mrs Duncan dies, her secret evidence left by her dead husband will end it all for the syndicate. Lagana, Stone, and all the other hoodlum cronies will be brought to justice, and it will be all over. This is where Debby becomes the avenging angel, once tainted goods in the eyes of society, a bad girl, she becomes the very thing that Bannion can't become, the one who implements absolute justice, an eye for an eye evenhandedness, and Bannion's unspoken partner to fix the wrong with the right. Debby visits Mrs Duncan on her own, and chit-chats her way into her house looking almost identical in matching mink coats, Mrs Duncan thinks Debby is a bit odd and is going to call Debby's boyfriend, Vince Stone, to come get her, but Debby pulls out the same gun Bannion left for her protection against the mob, and she shoots Mrs Duncan three times, making sure she is dead.

Bannion is determined to have it out with Stone, he waits outside and down the street until Stone returns to his plush apartment complex, and then Bannion follows him up the building. Stone nonchalantly takes his coat off and enters his living room in the dark, where he is instantly hit with boiling coffee upon his face.

Film Noir: The Best of The Classics

Debby turns on the light, still holding the pot of boiling coffee; she taunts Stone on how good the scar is going to look, especially in public as the people stare at him. She informs him its all over, Mrs Duncan is dead, the secret will be out, and Lagana's whole crime organization is ruined. Stone pulls out his gun and shoots her just as Bannion breaks into his apartment. A climatic gunfight ensues as they shoot at each other onto the huge balcony. The fight continues bare handed, Bannion beats Stone down, and points his gun at him, ready to kill him once and for all, but stops himself. Honorable police arrive and arrest Stone, Debby lies dying, and for the very first time, Bannion talks to her like a friend. He has come back to his humanity, with Debby's help, and justice is served. Through a terrible cost, the loss of so many lives, especially those of women, have paid an awful price, to rid the wickedness of the city and return it back to a safe heaven once again.

Austrian director Fritz Lang has been noted as being exemplary in film noir by utilizing his stark visual style and moody representation of human characters, and has a history of making great classics such as *Metropolis* (1927), *M* (1931), *Fury* (1936), and *The Big Heat* (1953). Lang came to America to escape the rise of Nazi power in Germany in 1934, he was part of the German expressionist, and could skillfully direct drama-thrillers and epic science fiction dramas with ease, as noted by Foster Hirsch in his book, *The Dark Side of the Screen: Film Noir*, "Of the four major Germanic directors of noir - Fritz Lang, Robert Siodmak, Billy Wilder, and Otto Preminger - Lang is the most consistently incisive. In temperament, he is the quintessential noir stylist" (Hirsch 116). Lang had a longstanding career in Hollywood, making numerous films of many genres, and seems to focus on the human perspective of outcomes that are beyond their control. "Lang's output over a period of almost forty years reveals a remarkable visual and thematic continuity. The director's noir titles - *The Ministry of Fear, The Woman in the Window, Scarlet Street, Human Desire, The Big Heat, Beyond a Reasonable Doubt* are a representative sampling - share strong thematic parallels. All concern victims of fate" (Hirsch 116).

    This is essentially the setting in *The Big Heat* that is full of victims in an era that is ripped right out of the news headlines making this a complex film noir that illustrates the advancement of organized crime in the 1950s, not just hoodlums trying to make a fast buck as during the Great Depression in the 1930s, the new generation of gangsters have gone corporate, by corrupting society by infiltration of businesses, law enforcement, and the legal system, and turning citizens into crooked pawns, as John Grant notes this in his book, *A Comprehensive Encyclopedia of Film Noir: The Essential Reference Guide*, "A sort of tour de force of many of noir's major themes" (Grant 65). Lang shoots the whole movie in a rather clean, crisp approach, without dramatic shadows, or noir stark lighting, but an almost documentary-style, contemporary film.

    The Big Heat was originally written in 1953 by William P. McGivern, a screenwriter and novelist who's forte was crime thrillers and murder mysteries, many of his books were adapted into films like *The Big Heat* (1953), *Rogue Cop* (1954), and *Odds Against Tomorrow* (1959), all these encompass that film noir quality that Hollywood studios at the time were looking for. McGivern also wrote the thriller screenplay for the film *I Saw What You Did* (1965), starring Joan Crawford and John Ireland. McGivern wrote over 20 novels, some of his most well-known are, *Caper of the Golden Bulls* (1964), *Choice of Assassins* (1965), *Night of the Juggler* (1974), and *Soldiers of '44* (1979). He also wrote scripts for TV shows such as Ben Casey (1961 - 1966), *Adam-12* (1968 - 1975), and *Kojak* (1973 - 1978).

    Sydney Boehm, former newspaper reporter turned screenwriter and producer, wrote the screenplay for *The Big Heat*. He could write for any genre he set his mind to, including westerns, action, thrillers, and science fiction. His most popular work is *Side Street* (1949), *When Worlds Collide* (1951), *The Big Heat* (1953), and *Secret of the Incas* (1954). Boehm was nominated for an Academy

Film Noir: The Best of The Classics

Award in 1953 for Best Writing, Story and Screenplay for *The Atomic City* (1952), he won the Edgar Allan Poe Award in 1954 (shared with for William P. McGivern), for Best Motion Picture for *The Big Heat* (1953). As a news reporter Boehm could interject a sense of realism into the script for *The Big Heat* by playing on the real life drama displayed on the news media and frantic law enforcement's efforts to rid the rampant organized crime in the 1950s.

The film has classic noir themes, only this time, the hard-boiled detective is actually a police detective turned cynical in his obsession to bring down the mob that has taken over the city. Bannion's conflict is with Lagana and Stone, what they stand for as murderers and thieves. Bannion's rough treatment with suspects accelerates, especially after they murder his wife, equally matched by the violence displayed by the very people he seeks to arrest. He teeters on the edge with a dispassionate glare during the entire movie. "Although designed as a contest between one brutality and another, Bannion's versus Stone's, the movie becomes a sort of psychological (and eventually physical) duel between Debby and Stone, with Grahame and Marvin emerging as the piece's stars rather than the rather wooden leading man Ford" (Grant 65).

The investigating hero is Det. Sgt. Dave Bannion (Glenn Ford), in *The Big Heat*; he is not only trying to stop criminals, but seeking justice for the murder of his wife. His emotional tone is more intense than say a streetwise detectives Marlowe or Spade, who are both more cool-headed, Bannion is out for personal reasons, vengeances, and causing the most harm as possible to his nemesis. Canadian born actor, Glenn Ford, is an exceptional actor with a long film career. "He rose to fame after serving in World War II, with roles alongside actresses Bette Davis and Rita Hayworth. Ford's career began in 1939 and continued well into the 1990s, including the 1957 film *3:10 to Yuma* and a small role in the original *Superman* (1978) film. In addition to acting in more than 100 films, Ford continued his military career in the US Naval Reserve" (biography).

T.S.Garp

Ford is a personal favorite actor of mine, some of his other film roles that go unnoticed, but are really interesting are *The Man from the Alamo* (1953), *The Fastest Gun Alive* (1956), *Jubal* (1956), and *Experiment in Terror* (1962). "(Ford) went on to establish his reputation as an actor capable of playing lead roles across various genres, including westerns, dramas and romantic films. His many films included *Gilda* (1946), with Rita Hayworth, *The Big Heat* (1953), *Blackboard Jungle* (1955), *The Teahouse of the August Moon* (1956), *The Courtship of Eddie's Father* (1963) and *Heaven with a Gun* (1969). From the 1970s, he appeared mainly in supporting roles in television series" (biography).

Film noir is no stranger to the viciousness of its characters upon each other nor in displaying odd surroundings (warehouses, old buildings, fancy apartments, urban homes, mansions, and theatres) mixed equally with ordinary environments where mayhem and murder can happen, "Bizarre backgrounds encourage the splashy visual set-pieces that decorate the genre. Usually involving a chase, a murder, a showdown, a release of tension or violence, a moment of madness; Lee Marvin throwing scalding coffee in Gloria Grahame's face in *The Big Heat*" (Hirsch 86).

Legendary great actor Lee Marvin, in one of his early acting roles, plays the vicious Vince Stone character in *The Big Heat*. "Having started out portraying sadistic bad guys in a number of notable film noirs, actor Lee Marvin was propelled to stardom and leading man status following his Oscar-winning performance as two characters in the classic Western comedy *Cat Ballou* (1965). Prior to that particular triumph, Marvin began making a name for himself with supporting roles in *The Wild One* (1953) and *The Big Heat* (1953), with the latter showcasing a famed scene where his menacing character threw scalding coffee in Gloria Grahame's face. Later in the decade, he had a stint as an investigator of organized crime on the briefly popular *M Squad* (NBC, 1957-1960), which helped turn the actor into star. Following turns as a sadistic cowboy in *Bad Day at Black Rock* (1955), the titular murderer in *The Man Who Shot Liberty Valence* (1962), and a

Film Noir: The Best of The Classics

methodical assassin in *The Killers* (1964), Marvin changed the course of his career with his Academy Award-worthy performance in *Cat Ballou*. From there, Marvin portrayed characters whose inescapable use of violence was nonetheless heroic" (TCM). One of my top Lee Marvin picks is a film where he uses no words to convey his meaning or emotional state, just action, in the violent crime film, *Point Blank* (1967) as Walker, directed by John Boorman.

Gloria Grahame (1923 - 1981) as the ill-fated Debby Marsh in *The Big Heat* is ideally portrayed by Grahame in a good-girl gone bad by choosing the wicket side of life, and ultimately paying the price for liking the wrong man, who is essentially good (Bannion). "Gloria Grahame likewise introduced a new shading to the fatal woman type, playing her not as a victimizer, a cruel tyrant, but as a victim, whimpering and aching and even good-hearted. (Hirsch 157). Grahame had an extraordinary career in Hollywood as, "a femme fatale with extraordinary carnal allure, Gloria Grahame electrified moviegoers with her turns as venal, sexually aggressive women in such films as *Crossfire* (1947), *In a Lonely Place* (1950) and *The Bad and the Beautiful* (1952), which earned her a Best Supporting Actress Oscar. A professional actress from childhood, Grahame began her career playing sexually confident if emotionally unstable women, and essentially repeated that role throughout the 1940s and 1950s, which marked her heyday in Hollywood. Few actresses could present such an openly wanton image as Grahame, whose heavy-lidded eyes and permanently curled lip - the result of botched surgery - lent her a physical gravitas other actresses lacked. Her women were dangerous, without question, and potentially lethal if cornered, like her mob moll in *The Big Heat* (1953), who lurked through the film's shadowy underworld on a hell-bent mission to avenge her disfigurement by Lee Marvin" (TCM).

I first saw Grahame on an episode of the original *Outer Limits* television series, *The Guests* (1964), where she played a forgotten film star living in the past, which some say Grahame was spoofing her own fading career in the 1960s. Nevertheless, "Grahame brought a note of pathos to noir. No one else projected quite the same combination of traits - dumb, sullen, devoted, available, hungry, above all steamy" (Hirsch 157). Another of Lee Marvin's other victims in *The Big Heat*, besides Bannion's wife or Debby Marsh (Gloria Grahame), was Doris (Carolyn Jones), she was badly burned briefly by Stone's cigar. Carolyn Jones was later nominated for an Academy Award for Best Supporting Actress for *The Bachelor Party* (1957) and a Golden Globe Award as one of the most promising actresses of 1959. However, she is best remembered as Morticia Addams on TV starring in *The Addams Family* (1964), receiving a Golden Globe Award nomination for her work.

The film *The Big Heat* is very different from other standard film noirs of the past, visually the style is more akin to regular filmmaking, but it's the sheer content of violence of all characters involved in the plot of the film that makes it a classic film noir crime-thriller. "Here is where noir comes into its own, introducing themes of true moral and psychological complexity. *Cornered, The Blue Dahlia, Black Angel, Phantom Lady, Deadline at Dawn, D.O.A., The Big Clock, The Big Heat* are stories of manhunts conducted by investigators with personal motives" (Hirsch 173). This is an excellent brutal crime drama that demonstrated a real threat, back in the 1950s with dealing with the national crime cartel.

The lead, Glenn Ford, is usually more expressive in other roles he has played, but nonetheless, he does a good job here as a cop working outside the law's confines, his obsession with the mob boss Lagana and sidekick, Stone, and the sorrow of over the death of his beloved wife, almost disregards his humanity at all the violence around him, that he becomes an unwilling example of someone pushed too far over the edge to reciprocate the same kind of violence he has pledged to stop. This is a great film on the themes of vengeance and justice, of Debby's and Bannion's, two lost souls seeking retribution in a cruel world controlled by organized crime. One of Fritz Lang's best American films, *The Big Heat*, is worth watching several times, for the German expressionism, the motives of vengeance for victims, and stark photography, all work so well in this film noir.

13

THE BIG COMBO

By the 1950s America's economy and social conscious had stabilized into a thriving upwardly mobile society. *The Big Combo* arrived during the declining years of classic film noir, instead of a hard-boiled detective trying to outwit a charming murderess, "the contrasting, late noir tendency is exaggeration tinged with satire. Such films as *Kiss Me Deadly*, *The Big Combo*, *Screaming Mimi*, *Touch of Evil*, all represent noir's decadence" (Hirsch 202). There are two opposing forces in *The Big Combo*, that of Police Lt. Diamond and gangster Mr. Brown, Diamond is fixated on putting away Mr. Brown behind bars for murder and all his other illegal dealings, but is that really the reason, as Grant clearly observes the main focus of the plot is centered around Diamond and Mr. Brown's girlfriend, "Mr. Brown (Conte, in a career-defining role), head of the local mob, The Combination - the "big combo" of the title. But is Diamond motivated entirely by a sense of justice, or is he responding instead to his desire for Susan Lowell" (Grant 64).

Despite *The Big Combo* being an entertaining movie with some twist and unexpected maneuvers by certain characters, the film noir genre operates best when dealing with a set formula of crime, murder, and greed, with taking enter stage of flawed tough men coupled with diabolical femme fatales and the era of disillusionment of the 1930s and 1940s, and as Hirsch points out, "one of the eroding factors in the fifties thrillers surfaced in such films as *The Big Combo* and *The Phenix City Story* where crime no longer springs form the aberrant individual but is instead a corporate enterprise, run like a business" (Hirsch 200). The film noir style was slowly fading by the late 1950s, having lost the postwar edge and confusion of society that dominated America when *The Maltese Falcon* (1941) was released.

The opening scene of *The Big Combo* begins with an overhead shot above the vast metropolitan city, composed of skyscrapers, cars, neon lights, and roving pedestrians. Cut to a boxing match in the heart of the city, during the fight we see an attractive blonde lady (Jean Wallace) suddenly running for her life, darting down dark corridors, searching for a way out, as two men chase her. This scene sets up how the rest of the film is going to look, full of dark, eerie lighting mixed with heavy shadows, all of which conveying a forbidding and desperate plight of the characters depicted in the film. *The Big Combo* was directed by Joseph H. Lewis and cinematography by John Alton. The excellent and moody saxophone score used in *The Big Combo* was untypical for the noir genre, but nevertheless, enhanced the style of the film overall was by David Raksin.

The story shifts from the desperation of Susan Lowell (Jean Wallace) fleeing in the opening shot of *The Big Combo* from her hired watchdogs to Police Lt. Leonard Diamond (Cornel Wilde) working late in his office. He has been on a six month campaign to thwart his nemesis, the gangster Mr. Brown (Richard Conte). But his superior, Police Capt. Peterson (Robert Middleton), comes in and thinks Diamond is spending too much time and money trying to bring down the powerful crime lord. He also points out that Diamond is becoming too reckless by being obsessed with Mr. Brown's girlfriend, Susan.

Controlled and monitored at all times, Susan is living in a nightmare existence, whenever she goes out, chaperoned by two of Mr. Brown's henchmen, Fante (Lee Van Cleef) and Mingo (Earl Holliman), constantly. Finally frustrated, she attempts to kill herself by overdosing on pills and is taken to the hospital. Diamond had an undercover policeman, Detective Sam Hill (Jay Adler), following Susan, to keep tabs on her safety and activity. Diamond, rushes over to check on Susan in the hospital, and overhears her mumbling over and over the name, Alicia. This is where the mystery part of the story really begins as Diamond, working on a hunch that Alicia is someone important to Mr. Brown, someone in trouble or someone missing, someone who might have been already killed by Mr. Brown. This sudden tip gives Diamond enough speculation to continue investigating a case against the sadistic crime boss and eventually bring him to justice.

Diamond orders questioning for every known hood that works for Mr. Brown, in an effort to discover who Alicia is. With nothing turning up fast, an annoyed and tired Diamond, seeks solace from his friend Rita (Helene Stanton), a showgirl performer working in one of the local nightclubs. Meanwhile, Mr. Brown questions his girlfriend, Susan, as to what she told Diamond about Alicia. Susan acts cold and distant; she is disheartened by her damaging relationship with Mr. Brown, and wonders why she even stays with him. Susan is caught in a fatal attraction made of wealth, sex, and drugs with him, and the subversive Mr. Brown is well aware of his charm over her, and he uses seduction to subdue her. In a daring cinematic move, the camera remains entirely on Susan's face as she can feel Mr. Brown kissing her further and further below the neck, until he disappears completely (below camera shot), assuming he is making his way down to her waist as she subtly gasp at the implied pleasure of sex. This scene has been a cult favorite for its daring portrayal and been ridiculed by censor advocates. It still holds up as a powerful display of filmmaking during the heavily conservative era of the 1950s.

Diamond visits Rita at her work, she warns him to blow town, the mob heat is growing on him, and word is out that he is marked for a possible hit if he sticks around much longer. He ignores her, and is snatched instantly right outside Rita's club by Fante and Mingo. Diamond is thoroughly beaten and torture by Joe McClure (Brian Donlevy), chief hood of Mr. Brown, Fante, Mingo, and Mr. Brown himself. They later dump him at Capt. Peterson's apartment, drunk, and disorientated. After recovering from that ordeal, Diamond traces a lead of a known associate of Mr. Brown in hiding that might have some clues about Alicia. As it turns out, Alicia is Mr. Brown's missing wife, resumed dead or murdered. Alicia was last seen on a boat commanded by Nils Dreyer (John Hoyt), who now owns an expensive antique shop funded by Mr. Brown.

Film Noir: The Best of The Classics

Diamond's investigation proves that Mr. Brown and Alicia were riding Dreyer's boat with Mr. Brown's former mob boss, Grazzi, from Sicily. He speculated that both Alicia and Grazzi are still missing, and that Dreyer suddenly had to order a new anchor, because someone is at the bottom of the ocean with an anchor tied to them. Dreyer claims he knows nothing, Diamond leaves, and shortly thereafter, McClure kills Dreyer in the alleyway behind the antique shop. Mr. Brown is furious, but remains cool-headed at the death of Dreyer; he confronts McClure for acting too stupid, and reminds why McClure is just too weak to run the combo organization. McClure hates Mr. Brown emphatically, but does nothing at this time.

Finally, the police get a major break, they obtain the contents of Dreyer's safe deposit box, and discover a film negative of three people dated seven years ago taken on his boat, Dreyer titled the snapshot: Grazzi. As the police try to build a case on Mr. Brown for murder, Diamond confesses his love to Susan, and warns her to leave Mr. Brown for good, to save her, so as not to end up like Mr. Brown's missing wife, Alicia. Having seen the photograph supplied by Diamond of Alicia, Susan later confronts Mr. Brown, and he claims Alicia is alive and well with Grazzi. Mr. Brown is angry by Diamond's constant probing and totally jealous of his love for Susan. That night he sends over Fante and Mingo to Diamond's apartment to kill him once and for all. But the two thugs botch the job by accidentally murdering Rita, who was innocently waiting for Diamond to come home that night. Diamond is determined now than ever to stop Mr. Brown's illegal rampage across the city.

Susan had obtained another, more recent photo of Alicia rumored to be living in Sicily. She gives the photo to Diamond to help with the investigation, and it proves that Alicia is alive, but living in America under a different name. Diamond travels to meet her, and tries to convince her to come back, and help prosecute her husband for murder. But Alicia Brown (Helen Walker), is reluctant to go and deal with the horror of what she saw by her husband's hand. Back in the city, McClure sees an opportunity for revenge; he tries to arrange a coup against his former subordinate Mr. Brown. He makes plans to kill Mr. Brown using Fante and Mingo as backup, they seem to agree with McClure, and listen to his entire proposal. McClure takes Mr. Brown to an abandon aircraft hangar for a delivery drop, but this is a trick, for Fante and Mingo are also there waiting in the shadows to ambush Mr. Brown. But the ultimate betrayal begins, as they point their machine guns to the unsuspecting McClure, this act alone shows you just how cold and calculating these men are, and with no hesitation, they mercilessly kill McClure in a hail of bullets.

Back at the police station, Susan tries to persuade Alicia to help the police to put her husband behind bar. Alicia at first refuses, but reconsiders until she has a mental relapsed at the sight of Mr. Brown face to face once again. Several days go by and the two hoods, Fante and Mingo, are hiding out in a secret wine cellar underneath a hotel, above the police dragnet is in full force over the city in search of them both for three murders. They sit and wait for Mr. Brown to give them safe passage out of the city. Mr. Brown finally shows up with gifts of food and traveling/payoff money, he'll return once they have checked everything. Once Mr. Brown leaves, the anxious thugs break open the money box, it is booby trapped with a live hand grenade, and it explodes in their faces. But the police find Mingo barely alive, but his partner Fante is dead, he then confesses against Mr. Brown. Feeling the heat of the police net closing in around him, Mr. Brown kidnaps Susan.

Diamond again, ask for Alicia's help one last time in finding where her husband has gone. She reluctantly tells him about a place he may have gone to. Susan and Mr. Brown are waiting inside the hangar for his plane to land at the secret location, and take them out of the city. The fog is super dense, a revolving beacon light in the distance breaks through the fog every few seconds, and Mr. Brown is getting impatient. Very soon a dark car approaches from the fog, it is Diamond and the police, and they have him surrounded. A disembodied voice shouts out to Mr.

Film Noir: The Best of The Classics

Brown to give up, but Mr. Brown answers back with gunfire into the fog and creepy night. Once his bullets are all used up, Diamond walks right in to arrest him, throws him to two uniformed policemen that promptly drag him away to jail. The evil crime spree of the city is over and justice is served.

The film's director, Joseph H. Lewis, was one of America's most stylish directors of primarily of the B-movie variety with a career spanning over 30 years in Hollywood. Lewis began working professionally with a movie camera early on, "he acquired these skills working as a camera assistant in the 1920's (his aptitude for the work may have been from his optometrist father) and further honed them in the MGM editorial department in the early '30s. After that Lewis edited serials at Republic and served the remainder of his apprenticeship as second unit director. He was signed to a full directing contract by Universal in 1937" (imdb, bio). Lewis had that special quality the French called auteur, his ability to hold his unique creative vision despite studio limitations, "A master of expressive lighting, tight close-ups, tracking and crane shots and offbeat camera angles and perspectives, Lewis possessed an instinctive sense of visual style, which imbued even the most improbable of his B-grade westerns and crime melodramas" (imdb, bio).

Lewis made quite a few pictures as director between 1937 to 1958, "he helmed numerous low-budget westerns, action pictures and thrillers and is remembered for original mysteries *My Name Is Julia Ross* (1945) and *So Dark the Night* (1946) as well as his most-highly regarded feature, 1949's *Gun Crazy*, which spotlighted a desperate young couple (Peggy Cummins and John Dall) who embark on a deadly crime spree" (imdb, bio). Consider two of Lewis' best work, were *The Big Combo* and *Gun Crazy*, that most excellently showcase his artistic approach, and "the term 'style over content' fits director Joseph H. Lewis like a glove. His ability to elevate basically mundane and mediocre low-budget material to sublime cinematic art has gained him a substantial cult following among movie buffs. The Bonnie & Clyde look-alike *Gun Crazy*

(1950), shot in 30 days on a budget of $400,000, is often cited as his best film" (imdb, bio).

"The astonishing cinematography by John Alton is paced to reach a climax just as the movie does: Diamond approaches to arrest Brown in an aircraft hanger, and Susan directs a small spotlight on the hoodlum as he darts back and forth along a corrugated iron fence like a cockroach seeking crack through which to escape. Immediately after, as Diamond walks out through the hangar door into the fog and Susan hurries after, there's a finale that consciously echoes the close of *Casablanca* (1942) and yet has become iconographic in its own right" (Grant 64). Born in Hungary in 1901, when his parents immigrated to America, Alton started working at the Cosmopolitan Studios in New York; he later moved to Hollywood, and began his career as a lab technician for MGM in the 1920s, and slowly moved up to cameraman for Paramount; and B-studios like RKO, at the height of his career Alton won the Academy Award, with Alfred Gilks, for the film *An American in Paris* (1952).

Alton gained the reputation at MGM as a preferred lighting director, and his style can easily be seen on such films like *Father of the Bride* (1950) and particularly his first work in color film, *An American in Paris* (1951), other major films were *Designing Women* (1957), *The Brothers Karamazov* (1958), and *Elmer Gantry* (1960). Alton used clever lighting, right angles, shadows, and implied action to get the subtle message across to his audiences. When dealing with sex and studio, how to bypass the strict profanity and violence codes by using implied expression and witty camera angles was Alton's forte. Working together to achieve artistic goals, Lewis and Alton, expertly set up shots and angles to circumvent the studio heads from implementing censor action on *The Big Combo*, but they were criticized just the same for the brutality and sexual conduct of the characters in the film.

Philip Yordan wrote the screenplay for *The Big Combo*, some of his early screenplays were for films *The Chase* (1946), *Whistle Stop* (1946), *House of Strangers* (1949), *Houdini* (1953), *Broken*

Film Noir: The Best of The Classics

Lance (1954), *Johnny Guitar* (1954), *King of Kings* (1961), with an uncredited Ray Bradbury. Alton also contributed to *El Cid* (1961), *55 Days at Peking* (1963), *The Fall of the Roman Empire* (1964), and *Night Train to Terror* (1985). Alton was "Nominated for an Academy Award for Best Writing, Screenplay for *Detective Story* (1951), and for Best Writing, Original Screenplay for *Dillinger* (1945). Won an Academy Award for Best Writing, Motion Picture Story for *Broken Lance* (1954), which was actually a remake, reset in the West, of the earlier *House of Strangers*" (Wikipedia). I've seen several of his historical based films and some of my personal favorites are *King of Kings, El Cid, 55 Days at Peking,* and *The Fall of the Roman Empire.*

The obsessed Police Lt. Diamond over Susan and gangster Mr. Brown, is played by Cornel Wilde in *The Big Combo*, a legendary actor, screenwriter, producer, and director who's vast "acting career began in 1935, in which year he made his debut on Broadway. In 1936, he began making small, uncredited appearances in films. By the 1940s, he had signed a contract with 20th Century Fox, and by the mid-1940s he was a major leading man. He was nominated for the Academy Award for Best Actor for his performance in 1945's *A Song to Remember.* In the 1950s, he moved to writing, producing and directing films, but still continued his career as an actor" (Wikipedia). I've been aware of his work for years and a fan of such films like *The Greatest Show on Earth* (1952), *Beyond Mombasa* (1956), *Constantine and the Cross* (1961) *Sword of Lancelot* (1963), *The Naked Prey* (1965), *and Beach Red* (1967). For cult fans of science fiction, Wilde can also be seen on an episode of the *Night Gallery* (1971) and *Gargoyles* (1972), made for TV movie, and the rare exploitation shark film, *Sharks' Treasure* (1975).

Wilde had created his own film production company called Theodora Productions, which produced the film noir *The Big Combo* (1955). Wilde's real life wife, Jean Wallace, played Susan Lowell opposite him in *The Big Combo*. Jean Wallace, was a former model turned actress in 1941. Her roles with movie studios were mostly minor, until she married Wilde, who took it upon himself to help her become a better actress by writing and directing her in his own pictures. Richard Conte played the notorious Mr. Brown, a prolific actor making over 100 films in his lifetime. Conte has been in numerous B-movies and many classic film noirs like *Whirlpool* (1949), *House of Strangers* (1949), and *The Sleeping City* (1950). Conte is perfect for the role of suave Mr. Brown. Influential, well-dressed, and clever, the character of Mr. Brown is a deadly killer who uses other people to handle his dirty work, but his motivations are clearly defined, as Hirsch notes, "the racketeer, crazed by jealously and ambition, in *The Big Combo*. Conte has a rugged charm, no matter what kind of part he plays" (Hirsch 163). In the role of Mr. Brown, "Conte is a cunning manipulator of women, turning into a tyrant when he fails to get what he wants" (Hirsch 163).

Other notable actors in *The Big Combo* include Brian Donlevy, Lee Van Cleef, and Earl Holliman. I remember Donlevy as Professor Quatermass in the British science-fiction horror film *The Quatermass Xperiment* (*The Creeping Unknown*), also made in 1955, and *Enemy From Space* (1957) for Hammer Films. Before rising to stardom, Cleef had been in numerous thrillers as a villain and Westerns, but slowly making his mark with such films like *High Noon* (1952), *The Beast from 20,000 Fathoms* (1953), *Man Who Shot Liberty Valance* (1962), and starring roles in *For a Few Dollars More* (1965) and *The Good, the Bad and the Ugly* (1966). Holliman is a notable actor for his contribution in such classics as *The Bridges at Toko-Ri* (1954), *Forbidden Planet* (1956), *Giant* (1956), *The Rainmaker* (1956), *Gunfight at the O.K. Corral* (1957), *The Sons of Katie Elder* (1965), *Anzio* (1968), and on the 1970s TV show *Police Women* (1974).

I really did enjoy *The Big Combo* and the lighting by Alton and directing by Lewis. I had always heard of the film, but never seen if until this review. I was a bit impressed with the creative visuals and how the film evokes the classic film noir style. In the final moments of the film, we see Mr. Brown being taken away by the police, they eerily disappear into the fog to his awaited fate, and this is purely a spooky and landmark scene. But what really makes *The Big Combo* more interesting and intriguing is the very last shot of the movie as we see the dark silhouette of Diamond and Susan with the circling aviation beacon light piercing the thick fog, high above them, this is a great symbolism of two people seeking justice and redemption over a force of evil, now gone. This cinematic ending shot was another example of Alton's great work. "Today, regarded as one of noir's classics, on release *The Big Combo* was received rather halfheartedly in general, although Alton's work was singled out for praise" (Grant 64).

On a final note, every character comes in casting huge shadows on the wall, in a slightly absurd story, as if we're watching two plays in action, one real and one surreal. The plot of *The Big Combo* hangs on the clue to where Alicia is and the obsessive Diamond for both Susan and Mr. Brown's unknown future. This melodrama is not perfect, doesn't shy away from violence, murder, torture, betrayal, and even a hint of sex on screen that is certainly implied, but it does supply another version of raw film noir 1950s style, and has some of the best actors in it that do a credible job for the roles they have.

14

TOUCH OF EVIL

This film so impressive on many levels, from the very beginning to the shocking ending, this is a filmmaker's delight, and visually stimulating for the audiences. Storywise, once you get through the convoluted plot, there comes a greater impact, a stunning cinematic masterpiece from one of America's greatest directors, Orson Welles, directing one of his last Hollywood films. Recapturing the marvel and talent displayed by Welles' best and early film, the infamous *Citizen Kane* (1941) made almost twenty years before. Welles skillfully weaves the camera and actors through a maze of shadows, sounds, and light. The opening sequence of *Touch of Evil* (1958) is magnificently done, orchestrated in a clever, artistic crane shot, that follows the action from beginning to end, down on street level to high above the building tops, as noted by Foster Hirsch, author of *The Dark Side of the Screen: Film Noir*, "The famous bravura opening, Welles' camera cranes and tracks athletically through the thronged main street as the hero and his wife (Charlton Heston and Janet Leigh) move against the flow of traffic, creating visual tension that is echoed everywhere in the packed frame" (Hirsch 79).

The story starts at night during the honeymoon of Mike Vargas (Charlton Heston) and his new wife, Susan Vargas (Janet Leigh), in Los Robles, a sleazy border town, between America and Mexico. From the very first shot of the film, we see the hands of a bomber plant his explosive device inside a car, and runs away, with no clear view of his face. The camera rises above the street and rooftop in an extended crane shot that follows the car, across the busy street filled with atmospheric sounds of clubs and car radios as the car cruises down the active street.

Within the moving crowd of people crossing the street is Mike and Susan just as the car crosses over the border back onto American soil, and instantly blows up, killing the two passengers.

Film Noir: The Best of The Classics

Mayhem ensues as the police, District Attorney Adair (Ray Collins) and Al Schwartz (Mort Mills), and the local sheriff arrives on scene. The introduction of Police Captain Hank Quinlan (Orson Welles), stepping out of his car is a bulky, imposing, cigar smoking man, intimidating and both grotesque figure that quips, "Did they toss it in or was it planted ahead of time?" Police Sergeant Pete Menzies (Joseph Calleia) answers, "Who?" Quinlan response, "Whoever did it, you jackass." This sets the tone for Quinlan's sarcastic, dogmatic, racist, and detached disposition throughout the film.

Mike Vargas is a Mexican drug enforcement official, intrigued by the bomb case and Quinlan's "intuition-leg" telling him it was most likely dynamite that caused the explosion, stays on as an observer, much to the dislike of Quinlan. Simultaneously, Susan Vargas is harassed by the slippery nightclub owner, Uncle' Joe Grandi (Akim Tamiroff), the local crime boss, and Pancho (Valentin De Vargas), because her husband is working on a legal case to put Grandi's brother in jail. On the hunt for clues across the border to Mexico, Quinlan questions the women working at the strip club and inquire about the girl killed in the car bomb to Strip-Club Owner (Zsa Zsa Gabor). Quinlan strolls over to visit an old friend, Tanya (Marlene Dietrich), a sort of gipsy fortune teller.

The next morning, Mike Vargas drives out of town to deposit his wife in a new motel, but midway is called away by the investigating police force, and she is driven by Menzies to the Mirador Motel, managed by a strange and nervous night clerk (Dennis Weaver), and unbeknownst to her is owned by the Grandi family. As the investigation escalates and the more Vargas questions the unorthodox methods of Quinlan and his so-called "hunches" and decidedly working on a personal agenda rather then seeking the truth, the more Vargas doesn't trust him. Quinlan openly despises Mexicans in general, and regards Mike Vargas as butting in on his jurisdiction and mild competition in pursuing the bombing suspect.

In an extreme take without any cuts (over 5 minutes long), Quinlan, Vargas, and police investigating team invade the apartment of Manelo Sanchez (Victor Millan) and his live-in girlfriend Marcia Linear (Joanna Moore), who just happens to be the bombing victim's estrange daughter. She already has an attorney on call and he takes her away. Sanchez unfortunately gets harassed by Quinlan and roughly interrogated by him. Vargas left to make a fast call to his wife, but upon his return to the Sanchez's apartment, they arrest him for having two sticks of dynamite concealed in the bathroom. Immediately, Vargas suspects Quinlan of planting evidence, and starts an investigation on Quinlan's outstanding police arrest record. Could the beloved and lager-than-life Police Captain Hank Quinlan be a crooked cop garnishing illegal convictions? Quinlan decides to take drastic action against Vargas and makes a deal with Grandi to implement it.

A diabolical plan is set in motion to frame Vargas's wife, Susan, on drug related changes and murder. While totally alone in the motel, a gang of teenage thugs working for the Grandi family take over the motel grounds. The gang breaks into Susan's room, grab her by force, and a female gang member with implied lesbian aspects (Mercedes McCambridge) prepares what appear to be illegal drugs. It is unclear if she was raped, but the scene spark terror and hopelessness for Susan. Later, Susan's nude and unconscious body is taken to a sleazy hotel, own by Uncle' Joe Grandi, and lay to rest on a bed. Meanwhile, Quinlan enters the room to complete the plan by murdering Grandi in cold blood. This is the moment Quinlan becomes truly evil, descending into a horrendous, morbid form, and twisted version of good gone bad.

Vargas returns only to find his wife in jail on drug and murder charges. He vows to stop Quinlan, having already found circumstantial evidence about past false convictions, and now wants to obtain a confession somehow. Menzies is suddenly made aware of Quinlan's involvement with the murder of Grandi, the attack on Susan, and perhaps falsely arresting the wrong people for over 30 years. Disenchanted, he agrees to wear a wire, confront

Film Noir: The Best of The Classics

Quinlan, and obtain a confession. Quinlan, drunk and despondent, ask Tanya to read his future for him. She replies, "You haven't got any."

Menzies finds Quinlan at Tanya's home, lures him outside, and they take a long walk through a heavy dirt and industrial area. Vargas trails them in secret, hidden in the shadows, trying to get a good signal for recording, and through the labyrinth of stern debris and muck. But Quinlan suspects a trap, hearing the echo of his own voice nearby, he pulls out his gun and regrettably shoots Menzies, and flees, but Vargas gives pursuit. Quinlan slips and warns Vargas that he is going to kill him. Quinlan takes careful aim at Vargas, but Menzies is still alive, and fatally shoots Quinlan. He staggers around a few more steps, realizing that he has Menzies' blood on his hands, and finally collapses dead in the murky, polluted stream. That touch of evil has been extinguished.

The history of motion pictures shows us that during the 1950s, film noir was on the decline, at its height of creativity came *The Maltese Falcon* in 1941 and ultimately ended with *Touch of Evil* in 1958. Even so, having just relocated back to the United States after living in Europe for ten years, and given the chance to direct a *Touch of Evil*, Welles contributed a tour de force of filmmaking inspired by film noir themes, a master at storytelling, and cinematography techniques, he created a "looming, restless, hyperactive camera, a barrage of tilted, disfiguring angles, complex and self-infatuated patterns of shadows, exotic settings - the film explodes as a series of visual fireworks, the syntax of noir slashed and then reconstructed as if for the last time" (Hirsch 11).

Multitalented, Orson Welles (1915–1985) was famous as a director, producer, writer, and actor. Won the Oscar for Best Writing and Original Screenplay for *Citizen Kane* with Herman J. Mankiewicz, and nominated for Best Director and Best Actor in a Leading Role for *Citizen Kane*. To really appreciate Welles extraordinary early film work, some of his best films are listed here, *Citizen Kane* (1941), *The Magnificent Ambersons* (1942), *Jane Eyre* (1943), *The Stranger* (1946), *The Lady from Shanghai*

(1947), *Macbeth* (1948), *The Third Man* (1949), *Othello* (1952), *Touch of Evil* (1958), and *The Trail* (1962). "Welles' vision is drawn to powerful and power-seeking figures like Kane, Macbeth, Mr. Arkadin, the sheriff in *Touch of Evil*. But his men of destiny are ultimately defeated by destiny, cut down by the very excesses of personality that elevated them to positions of power" (Hirsch 124). In a twist of irony, this is exactly what happened to Welles own film career.

Welles began his career on Broadway as an actor and writer, later at age 23 he became famous on the radio at The Mercury Theatre on the Air in New York for creating a hauntingly realistic version of H.G. Wells' *War of the Worlds* broadcast on October 30, 1938 that scared a nation into thinking an actual Martian invasion was taking place. Welles produced live radio dramas at the independent repertory theatre from 1938 to 1940. "Even while drawing the ire of some of his listeners, the broadcast cemented Welles' status as a genius, and his talents quickly became a fascination for Hollywood. In 1940 Welles signed a $225,000 contract with RKO to write, direct and produce two films. The deal gave the young filmmaker total creative control, as well as a percentage of the profits, and at the time was the most lucrative deal ever made with an unproven filmmaker. Welles was just 24 years old. Success wasn't immediate. Welles started and then stopped an attempt at adapting Joseph Conrad's *Heart of Darkness* for the big screen. The daring behind that project paled in comparison to what became Welles' actual debut film: *Citizen Kane* (1941)" (Biography).

Welles had been living overseas in Europe for ten years and had returned to America to work on films, instantly he was offered a role in *Touch of Evil*, but the leading actor (Charlton Heston) thought he should direct the film, as John Grant elaborates in his book, *A Comprehensive Encyclopedia of Film Noir: The Essential Reference Guide*. "Welles got the job of directing *Touch of Evil* because of Heston, who, hearing Welles was to be his costar, urged Universal to make him director as well. Universal agreed, but only if the budget for the movie was kept artificially low and Welles himself worked for free. The actors thus had to work for a fraction of their normal rates; even so, Welles had no trouble finding his cast" (Gant 658). Notwithstanding, many people in show business at that time just wanted to work with Welles on anything creative, he was that popular. This production was going to be run independently by Welles, who despised studio producers taking control of a director's artistic work. He was a very meticulous director and writer, and did everything under budget and on time.

Welles cast some of his most famous friends like Joseph Cotton and Marlene Dietrich in cameo roles for the film. Welles was a maverick filmmaker, open for improvisation, as is demonstrated with the Mirador Motel Night Manager played by actor Dennis Weaver, giving him free range to be creative with the part. If you blink, you'll miss Zsa Zsa Gabor, as the Even Strip-Club Owner.

When Welles took over as director, he immediately thought the original script by Paul Monash that was based on the novel *Badge of Evil* (1956) by Whit Masterson, wasn't up to par, and needed a rewrite. Welles rewrote the entire screenplay, changing the location to Mexico (broader town Los Robles), altering characters (American detective becomes a Mexican narcotics official), and added a swifter narrative. He essentially, left the core idea of the corrupt policeman planting evidence to catch a suspected bomber intact, but added German Expressionism and film noir qualities to properly convey the story. He used the music by Henry Mancini, most famous for Blake Edward's The Pink Panther films (1963) and music for *It Came from Outer Space* (1953), *The Creature from the Black Lagoon* (1954), *The Glenn Miller Story* (1954), and *This Island Earth* (1955). The studio producers were happy with the changes and pleased by the impressive work thus far (rushes), and were ready to offer Welles a 4 picture deal.

Charlton Heston plays Mike Vargas, the Mexican drug officer in *Touch of Evil*, and one of Hollywood's top leading men. Heston, an accomplished actor since the 1940s, has done film noir before, *Dark City* (1950), directed by William Dieterle. Heston later worked in Cecil B. DeMille's *The Greatest Show on Earth* (1952). Heston often plays in epic movies because of his a commanding appearance and voice as an actor. He has played historical and Biblical characters like Andrew Jackson in *The President's Lady* (1953); Moses in *The Ten Commandments* (1956), El Cid Rodrigo de Vivar in *El Cid* (1961), John the Baptist in *The Greatest Story Ever Told* (1964), Michelangelo in *The Agony and the Ecstasy* (1965), General Charles Gordon in *Khartoum* (1966), and Cardinal Richelieu in *The Three Musketeers* (1973 - 1975). But he is also best remembered for his roles in *Touch of Evil* (1958), *Ben-Hur* (1959), *Will Penny* (1967), *Planet of the Apes* (1968), *The Omega Man* (1971), and *Soylent Green* (1973).

Janet Leigh played Susan Vargas, a fearless, devoted wife, and strong female character in the *Touch of Evil*. In real life, Leigh was as determined as her on screen character, "Leigh broke her arm just a couple of weeks before shooting started and removed her sling only when the cameras were rolling" (Gant 658). Leigh has been acting since the 1940s, in such memorable roles in *Little Women* (1949), *Houdini* (1953) with her then husband Tony Curtis, *The Vikings* (1958), *Psycho* (1960), *The Manchurian Candidate* (1962), and *The Fog* (1980) with her daughter Jamie Lee Curtis.

Orson Welles not only directed *Touch of Evil*, but he also plays the tyrant in the film. Police Captain Hank Quinlan (Orson Welles), a sad and tragic figure of a man consumed with power, hate, and revenge for the death of his wife some 30 years prior, but still a corrupted law enforcement official, nevertheless, turned evil. From the start, American test audiences in 1957 did not embrace the film, "The reason for this US disdain may be that the characterization of Quinlan perhaps struck a little too close for comfort" (Grant 658). The portrayal of a crooked cop might be an unpleasant thought, but there were other obvious reasons the film had a cold response, like the interracial marriage of Mike Vargas (Charlton Heston) and Susan Vargas (Janet Leigh), the undertone of racism, drug use, teenage delinquents, and rock music was all very risqué at the time. This might have been too much for

Film Noir: The Best of The Classics

American audiences to take in the conservative 1950s, avoiding issues of political scandals, war, and trying to maintain an optimistic outlook that is a complete opposite to the pessimistic viewpoint film noir had showcased in the 1940s.

Universal Studios felt the film was a disaster, unwatchable, and didn't make sense of the plot. Despite the fantastic collaboration of Welles and his cinematographer by Russell Metty, an expert on light and shadow, low angles and high, visual creator of atmospheric worlds, as demonstrated in films such as *The Stranger* (1946) and *Touch of Evil* (1958). The Producers fired Welles and ordered a new director, Harry Keller, to reshoot key scenes or add new ones, alter the music, narration, and re-edit the entire movie down to 95 minutes. The end result upon release in 1958 was that American audiences hated the film, "Though more or less ignored in the US, receiving minimal release, it had a much more favorable critical and commercial reception in Europe" (Grant 658). The film did not make any sense to American audiences and was chopped up so badly it lost its cohesion. This debacle ended Welles Hollywood film career and he slipped into obscurity thereafter.

This would have been an excellent film for Welles to make a comeback on, if he had made it ten years prior, but it was made far too late in the film noir era, film audiences had changed, and America was less cynical by the late 1950s. Nevertheless, Welles's insight into the story and the nature of the corrupt, leading character was a perfect match for film noir. "Stories of inveterate criminals (*White Heat*, *Touch of Evil*, *Night and the City*, *Night of the Hunter*) adhere more closely than the private eye or victim dramas to the Expressionist's nightmare world. These films veer, typically, from a detached view of madness to occasional hallucinatory renderings of the psychopath's disordered mind" (Hirsch 168). But the film was mishandled, butchered, and left for dead by Universal Studios.

I really enjoyed the elaborate and stylized shots, the violence undercut by satire, and Orson Welles' own visual sense is brilliant, almost intuitive, sense of filmmaking. This incredible film, *Touch of Evil,* despite being poorly altered by the studio heads has over time became a classic and cult favorite of professional filmmakers and fans all over the world. Film historians and enthusiast were eagerly searching for a lost original copy of Welles' final cut, and in 1975, UCLA film archives discovered a rare 108-minute version of the film, but not the complete Welles version. Interestingly enough and fortuitously for us, American film critic, Jonathan Rosenbaum published in 1997, Welles urgent memo to Universal executives to restore the film with his added revisions to make it whole again.

Thankfully, with Universal's go head, by 1998 a newly restored film was achieved by making some 50 structured and stylistic changes that reflect Welles wishes, and the results were phenomenal. The film critics loved it, finally seeing the film the way it was meant to be seen, making the plot easier to follow, maintaining the impressionistic style, and consistency. I was lucky enough to see the new 111-minute version of *Touch of Evil* for this review, I have been a fan of Orson Welles for many years, and seeing his masterpiece fully restored to his artistic vision is superb, and a testament to his genius and talent as a writer and director. To really appreciate Welles' as a filmmaker, one needs only to watch two of his films, *Citizen Kane* and *Touch of Evil.*

Bibliography

Grant, John. *A Comprehensive Encyclopedia of Film Noir: The Essential Reference Guide.* Milwaukee: Limelight Editions; 2013.

Hirsch, Foster. *The Dark Side of the Screen: Film Noir.* Boston: Da Capo Press; 2nd edition, 2008.

Spicer, Andre and Helen Hanson. *A Companion to Film Noir.* Hoboken: Wiley-Blackwell; 1 edition, 2013.

Filmography

The Big Combo. Director: Joseph H. Lewis. Producer: Sidney Harmon. Cast: Cornel Wilde, Richard Conte, Brian Donlevy, Jean Wallace, and Lee Van Cleef. Allied Artists., Theodora Productions, 1955.

The Big Heat. Director: Fritz Lang. Producer: Robert Arthur. Cast: Glenn Ford, Gloria Grahame, Jocelyn Brando, Alexander Scourby, and Lee Marvin. Columbia Pictures, 1953.

The Big Sleep. Director: Howard Hawks. Producer: Howard Hawks. Cast: Humphrey Bogart, Lauren Bacall, and John Ridgley. Warner Brothers, 1946.

Cat People. Director: Jacques Tourneur. Producer: Val Lewton. Cast: Tom Conway, Simone Simon, Jack Holt, Jane Randolph and Kent Smith. RKO Radio Pictures, 1942.

D. O. A. Director: Rudolph Maté. Producer: Leo C. Popkin. Cast: Edmond O'Brien, Pamela Britton, Luther Adler, Beverly Campbell-Garland, and Lynn Baggett. United Artists., Cardinal Pictures, 1950.

Detour. Director: Edgar G. Ulmer. Producer: Leon Fromkess. Cast: Tom Neal, Ann Savage, Claudia Drake, and Edmund MacDonald. Producers Releasing Corp., 1945.

Double Indemnity. Director: Billy Wilder. Producer: Joseph Sistrom. Cast: Fred MacMurray, Barbara Stanwyck, Edward G. Robinson, Porter Hall, and Jean Heather. Paramount, 1944.

Gun Crazy. Director: Joseph H. Lewis. Producers: Frank King and Maurice King. Cast: Peggy Cummins and John Dall. United Artists., King Brothers Productions, 1950.

In a Lonely Place. Director: Nicholas Ray. Producer: Robert Lord. Cast: Humphrey Bogart and Gloria Grahame. Columbia Pictures, 1950.

Kiss Me Deadly. Director: Robert Aldrich. Producer: Robert Aldrich. Cast: Ralph Meeker, Albert Dekker, Paul Stewart, Juano

Hernandez, and Gaby Rodgers. United Artists., Parklane Pictures, 1955.

The Maltese Falcon. Director: John Huston. Producer: Hal B. Wallis. Cast: Humphrey Bogart, Mary Astor, Peter Lorre, Sydney Greenstreet, and Elisha Cook Jr. Warner Bros. Pictures, 1941.

Out of the Past. Director: Jacques Tourneur. Producer: Warren Duff. Cast: Robert Mitchum, Jane Greer, Kirk Douglas, and Rhonda Fleming. RKO, 1947.

The Third Man. Director: Carol Reed. Producer: Alexander Korda. Cast: Joseph Cotten, Alida Valli, Orson Welles, Trevor Howard, and Bernard Lee. British Lion Film Corp., London Film Productions, 1949.

Touch of Evil. Director: Orson Welles. Producer: Albert Zugsmith. Cast: Charlton Heston, Janet Leigh, Orson Welles, Joseph Calleia, and Akim Tamiroff. Universal Studios, 1958.

Website Referenced

"A. I. Bezzerides." Wikipedia. Wikimedia Foundation, n.d. Web. 23 Oct. 2015. <https://en.wikipedia.org/wiki/A._I._Bezzerides>

Beaver, Jim. "Biography." Robert Mitchum. IMDb.com, n.d. Web. 18 Sept. 2015. <http://www.imdb.com/name/nm0000053/bio>.

"Benjamin H. Kline." TV.com. N.p., n.d. Web. 11 Sept. 2015. <http://www.tv.com/people/benjamin-h-kline/>

Bergan, Ronald. N.p., 28 Aug. 2001. Web. 25 Sept. 2015. <http://www.theguardian.com/news/2001/aug/28/guardianobituaries.filmnews>.

Bio.com. A&E Networks Television, n.d. Web. 30 Oct. 2015. <http://www.biography.com/people/glenn-ford-218196>.

Bio.com. A&E Networks Television, n.d. Web. 6 Nov. 2015. <http://www.biography.com/people/orson-welles-9527363>.

"Biography." Alida Valli. IMDb.com, n.d. Web. 27 Nov. 2015. <http://www.imdb.com/name/nm0885098/bio?ref_=nm_ov_bio_sm>.

"Biography for Charlton Heston." Turner Classic Movies. N.p., n.d. Web. 06 Nov. 2015. <http://www.tcm.com/tcmdb/person/85772|30940/Charlton-Heston/biography.html>.

"Biography." Jane Randolph. IMDb.com, n.d. Web. 13 Nov. 2015. <http://www.imdb.com/name/nm0709905/bio?ref_=nm_ov_bio_sm>.

"Cornel Wilde." Wikipedia. Wikimedia Foundation, n.d. Web. 02 Oct. 2015. <https://en.wikipedia.org/wiki/Cornel_Wilde>.

"Dorothy B. Hughes." Wikipedia. Wikimedia Foundation, n.d. Web. 03 Dec. 2015. <https://en.wikipedia.org/wiki/Dorothy_B._Hughes>.

"Edgar G. Ulmer." IMDb. IMDb.com, 17 Oct. 1990. Web. 10 Sept. 2015. <http://www.imdb.com/name/nm0880618/?ref_=fn_al_nm_1%3Emurder>.

"Ernest Laszlo Profile." Turner Classic Movies. N.p., n.d. Web. 24 Oct. 2015. <http://www.tcm.com/this-month/article/294369|0/Ernest-Laszlo-Profile.html>.

Fob, Frank. "Biography." Rudolph Maté. IMDb.com, n.d. Web. 10 Sept. 2015. <http://www.imdb.com/name/nm0005789/bio?ref_=nm_ov_bth_nm>.

Fob, Frank. "Robert Aldrich." IMDb. IMDb.com, n.d. Web. 25 Oct. 2015. <http://www.imdb.com/name/nm0000736/>.

"Howard Hawks." IMDb. IMDb.com, n.d. Web. 18 Sept. 2015. <http://www.imdb.com/name/nm0001328/>.

"Humphrey Bogart." IMDb. IMDb.com, n.d. Web. 16 Sept. 2015. <http://www.imdb.com/name/nm0000007/>.

"IEC." Rudolph Maté. N.p., n.d. Web. 11 Sept. 2015. <http://www.cinematographers.nl/GreatDoPh/mate.htm>.

"Jacques Tourneur." Wikipedia. Wikimedia Foundation, n.d. Web. 25 Sept. 2015. <https://en.wikipedia.org/wiki/Jacques_Tourneur>.

"Janet Leigh." IMDb. IMDb.com, n.d. Web. 24 Nov. 2015. <http://www.imdb.com/name/nm0001463/?ref_=fn_al_nm_1>.

"Joseph Cotton." Wikipedia. Wikimedia Foundation, n.d. Web. 26 Nov. 2015. <https://en.wikipedia.org/wiki/Joseph_Cotton>.

"Leigh Brackett." IMDb. IMDb.com, n.d. Web. 18 Sept. 2015. <http://www.imdb.com/name/nm0102824/?ref_=fn_al_nm_1>.

Mowis, I. S. "Biography." Joseph H. Lewis. IMDb.com, n.d. Web. 07 Oct. 2015. <http://www.imdb.com/name/nm0507390/bio>.

"Nicholas Musurac." Wikipedia. Wikimedia Foundation, n.d. Web. 25 Sept. 2015. <https://en.wikipedia.org/wiki/Nicholas_Musuraca>.

"Nicholas Ray." Wikipedia. Wikimedia Foundation, n.d. Web. 03 Dec. 2015. <https://en.wikipedia.org/wiki/Nicholas_Ray>.

"Overview for Gloria Grahame." Turner Classic Movies. N.p., n.d. Web. 28 Oct. 2015. <http://www.tcm.com/tcmdb/person/74987|62459/Gloria-Grahame/>.

"Overview for Kent Smith." Turner Classic Movies. N.p., n.d. Web. 12 Nov. 2015. <http://www.tcm.com/tcmdb/person/179849|93913/Kent-Smith/>.

"Overview for Lee Marvin." Turner Classic Movies. N.p., n.d. Web. 28 Oct. 2015. <http://www.tcm.com/tcmdb/person/123980|96650/Lee-Marvin/>.

"Philip Yordan." Wikipedia. Wikimedia Foundation, n.d. Web. 01 Oct. 2015. <https://en.wikipedia.org/wiki/Philip_Yordan>.

"Robert Krasker Profile." Turner Classic Movies. N.p., n.d. Web. 27 Nov. 2015. <http://www.tcm.com/this-month/article/499697|0/Cinematography-by-Robert-Krasker-10-13.html>.

"Russell Harlan Profile." Turner Classic Movies. N.p., n.d. Web. 07 Oct. 2015. <http://www.tcm.com/this-month/article/411172|412422/Russell-Harlan-Profile.html>.

"Russell Rouse." Wikipedia. Wikimedia Foundation, n.d. Web. 15 Oct. 2015. <https://en.wikipedia.org/wiki/Russell_Rouse>.

Seabrook, Jack. "Bare•bones E-zine." : Shatner Meets Hitchcock Part One: Alfred Hitchcock Presents "The Glass Eye" N.p., n.d. Web. 13 Nov. 2015. <http://barebonesez.blogspot.com/2012/07/shatner-meets-hitchcock-part-one-alfred.html>.

"Sydney Boehm." IMDb. IMDb.com, n.d. Web. 29 Oct. 2015. <http://www.imdb.com/name/nm0091213/>.

"Sidney Hickox." IMDb. IMDb.com, n.d. Web. 18 Sept. 2015. <http://www.imdb.com/name/nm0005741/>.

"The Big Sleep." SparkNotes. SparkNotes, n.d. Web. 17 Sept. 2015. <http://www.sparknotes.com/lit/bigsleep/context.html>.

Made in the USA
Lexington, KY
02 January 2018